Maida L. Riggs is Professor Emeritus, University of Massachusetts at Amherst, and has over twenty years of experience observing and participating in nursery school programs in the United States, Great Britain, Holland, Germany, Australia, New Zealand, and the USSR. She is a noted lecturer, writer, and authority in the field of physical education, early childhood, and development.

JUMP

Maida L. Riggs

Photographs by
University of Massachusetts Photo Center
and Cynthia Buck

TO JOY

Helping Children Grow
Through Active Play

A SPECTRUM BOOK

Prentice-Hall Inc., Englewood Cliffs, N.J. 07632

Library of Congress Cataloging in Publication Data

Riggs, Maida L
  Jump to joy.

  (A Spectrum Book)
  Bibliography: p.
  Includes index.
  1. Movement education. 2. Motor ability in children.
3. Motor learning. I. Title.
  GV452.R53   613.7′042   80-11795
  ISBN 0-13-512343-7
  ISBN 0-13-512335-6 (pbk.)

Quote on p. 76 is reprinted from E. B. Castles, *The Teacher* (Oxford, England: Oxford University Press, 1970). Quote on page 108 is reprinted with permission of Penguin Books, Ltd., from Susanna Millar, *The Psychology of Play* (London: Pelican Books, 1968), pp. 125–26; copyright © Susanna Millar, 1968.

To the children of the North Village Children's Center

Jump to Joy: Helping Children Grow through Active Play by Maida L. Riggs.
© 1980 by Prentice-Hall, Inc., Englewood Cliffs, N.J. 07632

A SPECTRUM BOOK

Printed in the United States of America

10 9 8 7 6 5 4 3 2 1

Editorial/production supervision and interior design by Maria Carella.
Manufacturing buyer: Cathie Lenard.
Art Director: Jeannette Jacobs.

PRENTICE-HALL INTERNATIONAL, INC., *London*
PRENTICE-HALL OF AUSTRALIA PTY., LIMITED, *Sydney*
PRENTICE-HALL OF CANADA, LTD., *Toronto*
PRENTICE-HALL OF INDIA PRIVATE, LIMITED, *New Delhi*
PRENTICE-HALL OF JAPAN, INC., *Tokyo*
PRENTICE-HALL OF SOUTHEAST ASIA PTE., LTD., *Singapore*
WHITEHALL BOOKS, LIMITED, WELLINGTON, *New Zealand*

Contents

v

Preface

Jump to Joy is a book about children from ages 2½ through 5 who are involved in purposeful motor experiences. These activities are applicable to older children as well. The book includes a discussion of the children's physical and neuromuscular growth and development patterns, as well as a description of specifically designed movement activities in the gymnasium, playground, or backyard in which they may engage to enhance their psychomotor, cognitive, and affective development. The book is also about the people who teach them—those physical educators, parents, aides, and playground directors, who have been specially trained to understand the significance of motor development for young children. Included as well is a discussion of the role of those nursery-school and kindergarten teachers, aides, and parents whose focus is also on the importance of motor development.

Personal experiences are always important in one's writing, and I have drawn extensively from mine, both as a child and from working with young children. I was fortunate to have had a childhood packed full of play opportunities—a large play yard; parents who created playful experiences and provided for playthings; a tolerant, loving mother and grandmother who let me play house on rainy days; and a father who bought or built large climbing apparatus. And I lived in the country where there were birches to swing from, railroad tracks to balance on, and challenging trees to climb—conditions that can be simulated in the gymnasium or playground for the urban child.

In this book I have attempted to bring together knowledge of all aspects of child development, with special emphasis on motor development, in such a way that young teachers and parents may choose to work with this age group because they, too, will appreciate its significance and will be able to see the rapid increase in psychomotor skill, more acute intellectual functioning, and enhanced emotional performance that follow these movement experiences. Children of this age are exciting to teach because they are normally so uninhibited, full of energy, divergent in their thinking, spontaneous, self-motivating, curious, and so happy. It is these characteristics of abundant energy, joy in moving, openness, agility, powers of observation and imitation, and alertness that my students and I seek to preserve while providing the children with opportunities to develop the fundamental psychomotor skills that are so important at this age. I believe that free activity and its ancillary, self-discovery, are complementary to the way children learn and that they release and strengthen these characteristics.

The longer I teach, the more important these younger years seem to be. Having begun working with preschool children in a formal way about fifteen years ago, I am convinced of the wisdom of providing them with an enriched environment where learning may be elicited and/or facilitated. I am aware of the time and energy cost factors involved in trying to teach young children before they are maturationally ready, but after twenty years of observation and participation in nursery schools in the United States, Great Britain, Holland, Germany, Australia, New Zealand, and the Soviet Union, I am also aware of the lack of attention paid to the development of gross motor skills, both in the schools themselves and in literature about young children. In most instances there is plenty of opportunity for fine motor development, with the use of scissors, crayons, finger paints, and clay; but provision for large muscle activity, although there is some climbing apparatus, is largely left to chance. The professional literature that concerns itself with child development either gives token attention to it or completely avoids coming to grips with this most important, most pervasive aspect of development. The recent decision to close nursery schools in Great Britain suggests that many educators do not share my belief in the importance of these early years for learning.

It is also because I believe that these are formative years in other domains as well, and that the kind of activities that my students and I plan for young children contribute to the skills of these domains, that I find this work exciting. I believe that it encourages young children to take more initiative, to become more autonomous and therefore more constructive individuals, that I find it so rewarding. I believe, too, that with this kind of self-fulfilling activity as young children, there develops a very great positive attitude toward physical activity as an intergral part of living. It is probably the emotional component of pleasure that acts as the cement for cognitive and psychomotor development. It is important to ensure that such a positive relationship is maintained.

This book is intended as an introductory text. It represents a distillation of information from a wide variety of disciplines mediated through my experience with children, which has directed and dictated what needs to be known in order to create an environment that enhances and facilitates their total development. Research by Halvorson (1966),* and Sinclair (1973) has determined how children of specific age ranges perform certain motor tasks; it has not looked at the benefits of an enriched psychomotor environment and how these skills or tasks would change under such conditions. Research has been more interested in describing what children do—that is, how they perform now—rather than how well they might perform in an environment that is structured to enhance or facilitate psychomotor development.

When working in the psychomotor domain, it would be helpful if we could demonstrate that some of the positive relationships between improved motor and intellectual performance that are advanced are statistically significant, as the work of Bruner (1976) does. Children of this age, in this setting, in numbers as large as my students and I have had, do not lend themselves to some of the measuring devices or tight research designs necessary for statistically significant results. These children are involved in what Piaget (1961) calls "Mastery Play" when he says: "This activity is no longer an effort to learn, it is only a happy display of known actions" (p. 166). Perhaps a better term for what happens in the gymnasium is the practice of emerging skills. There has been no attempt to measure the

*Full citations for references in the Preface are given at the end of the book.

distance of a jump or the speed of a run—only to ensure that children do jump, jump, jump and run with the freedom and speed of wind.

With full recognition and acceptance that each person responds as a "total being," I have deliberately resorted to the Greek notion of the tripartite nature of humanity and consider the three parameters of development, thoughts, and feelings and actions separately. Because there is a strong reciprocal relationship between having fun (affective) and remembering (cognitive), there is a concerted attempt to ensure that the activities included are those for which children have very positive feelings, as they do for things that move. To look at the children's happy faces, one feels that it is the emotional component that acts to bind cognitive and psychomotor development together. Part I of the book is, therefore, a discussion of children who are involved in purposeful activity in the gymnasium, playground, or backyard and the contributions this activity makes to their total development.

There are always two other facets to the formal learning environment—the teacher, and the educational setting or equipment, which, in this case, is large gymnastic apparatus and small manipulative equipment such as balls, scooters, and hoops. In Part II I have chosen to look in detail at the skills that are necessary if a teacher, parent, aide, camp counselor, or playground director is to work successfully with children of this age, in these settings. The roles that responsible adults play in the gymnasium are essentially the same as those in the nursery-school setting, with the major exception that knowledge of large apparatus and the kinds of activities it invites and promotes is mandatory. In this sense it takes a very specially trained teacher to set up and supervise a challenging, yet safe, environment. Parents, aides, and playground directors can be those specially trained people. Knowledge of motor skills, their developing patterns, and ways to evoke them becomes a very special tool in the hands of this teacher. It is because I believe that we need to train more teachers and parents to become competent at working with young children, and that it takes a rather special person to act in this responsible capacity, that I feel this section of the book is very important.

Part III focuses on the prerequisites for the gymnasium and/or playground itself and uses of the apparatus. The gymnasium happens to be the setting in which I have worked, but the comments about apparatus and the activities under discussion in this book are applicable to the backyard and playground as well. Children love to run, swing, jump, and climb, so certain pieces of apparatus will always challenge them. They have taught me how high they like to go, how often they will jump, and from how many parts of their body they can swing. And so I wish to share many of the ways my students and I have found to challenge young children and what fun it is to see the different ways they choose to use apparatus.

Above all, I hope that some of the enthusiasm I feel for working with young children will be transmitted to the reader.

The author's primary indebtedness is to the children of the North Village Children's Center who inspired and provided hands-on material for this book. The persistence of their teachers, David Zuccalo and Marie Haemer, that the children be permitted to engage in a biweekly period of gross motor activity, enabled physical education and early childhood major students at U. Mass/Amherst to have a firsthand experience in observation and responsibility for pre-school children. Carolyn Carlson, U. Mass Photo Center, and Cynthia Buck, Tripod and Easel Studio, have captured the joy and range of movement activities that young children discover when presented with developmentally appropriate, challenging equipment and supportive teachers.

MAIDA L. RIGGS
Hadley, Massachusetts

Children are our most valuable resource for the future.

THE DEVELOPMENT
OF PURPOSEFUL
MOVEMENT:
The Children

1

Introduction

Skilled behavior is not just organized.
It is organized with a purpose.
*It is goal-directed.**

Humanity's uniqueness includes at least three major characteristics that distinguish people from animals: *upright locomotion,* with its attendant mechanical changes in posture; *manipulative skills and visual apparatus* accommodated to the postural change; and *speech,* with its accompanying changes in social skills and practices. These human differences, according to Rosenbloom (1975), provide four major parameters of human development:

*From Paul M. Fitts and Michael Posner, *Human Performance* (Belmont, CA.: Brooks/Cole Publishing Company, 1968).

3

Day-care center, North Village, Amherst, Massachusetts. A shady place to play on a summer day.

Motor: involving body postures and large movements with a high level of physical competence and economy of effort.

Vision and fine movements: involving visual perception (near and far) and manipulation.

Hearing and speech: hearing and listening competence and the use of speech and language.

Social behavior and spontaneous play: involving competence in organization of self-identity, self-care, and progressively effectual self-occupation in conjunction with increasing voluntary acceptance of social standards (i.e., personal relations, cultural demands).*

The major focus of Part I is on motor development, and in its consideration, the first three parameters just mentioned are intrinsically interdependent. All gross body movements depend upon the integration of sensory information derived from visual, auditory, vestibular, and proprioceptive sources. Although vision is a dominant sense for most of the information we process from the environment, children of these ages acquire most of their language as well as learning about what they should or should not do through what they hear. Knowledge about what the body

*Lewis Rosenbloom, "The Consequences of Impaired Movement; A Hypothesis and Review," in Kenneth Holt, *Movement and Child Development*, Clinics in Developmental Medicine No. 55 (Philadelphia: J. B. Lippincott, 1975).

is doing, the position of its parts—especially with regard to gravity—is derived from both the vestibular apparatus—located adjacent to the inner ear—and the proprioceptors—which are specialized sense organs within the muscles, tendons, and joints.

Since the major thrust of Part I is to deal with the development of gross movements, these four senses and their relationship are examined. It is not within the scope of this book to present a detailed study of kinesiology, the visual and auditory apparatus, or the development of speech, although these certainly have motor aspects. References are supplied at the end of the book that provide a basis for more in-depth study. The scope of this part of the book is to integrate knowledge of motor development with knowledge of the needs of young children.

It is the author's contention that socialization and/or play are vital vehicles for, and the result of, gross motor development. It is of sufficient importance, therefore, to consider the subject of play in some detail. Since children spend most of their waking time during their first five years playing, we shall look at the contributions of play to neuromuscular development. When involved in large muscle activity, children of this age appear to be particularly egocentric, and the process of playing with others has not been one of their major objectives. However, the opportunity to help others, to take turns, is there for the children who are ready.

What contributions does involvement in purposeful physical activity

Excellent backyard equipment. Child Life Play Specialties, Inc., Holliston, Massachusetts.

Puzzlement: "What do I do next?"

make to cognitive and affective growth during this time? What physical and physiological changes are taking place in the body at this age to permit vigorous activity, and what contributions does vigorous activity make to these changes? These are some of the questions we, who have been actively engaged in working with young children, are asking.

First let us develop an understanding of the factors involved in neuromuscular development and then study its contributions to, and significance for, total development. Young children are experimenting with what the body can do (subject); we are interested in what happens to the body (object) as well.

References

LEWIS ROSENBLOOM, "The Consequences of Impaired Movement; A Hypothesis and Review." In Kenneth Holt, *Movement and Child Development* (Philadelphia: J.B. Lippincott Co., 1975).

2

Neuromuscular Development

It is during the early years that the basic patterns of locomotion, manipulation, and language behavior are developed. *

Neuromuscular development may be described as occurring along a continuum, those reflex forms that ensure survival on one end and the most automated forms of movement on the other. As the central nervous system takes over, one can observe movement change into complex, volitional, automated patterns represented by expression, such as dance, competition, running fast, enjoyment, and jumping rope or the functional acts of getting about at school or play. This development is largely a function of age; that

*From Paul M. Fitts and Michael Posner, *Human Performance* (Belmont, CA.: Brooks/Cole Publishing Company, 1968).

is, the older one becomes, in general, the more automated is one's behavior. However, researchers are only just beginning to look at the effect of experience on neuromuscular development. Holle (1976) summarizes the changes in neurological development that result in volitional or automated movement:*

1. Reflex activity: The neonate has no cortical control over the lower centers of the brain.
2. Symmetrical activity: Brain control is beginning.
3. Voluntary activity: The central nervous system is now able to initiate as well as to inhibit movement.
4. Automatic: Movement becomes habitual. (p. 8)

Perhaps some of these terms need amplification. Prenatal and neonatal movement is mainly reflex in nature; that is, it involves the simplest functioning unit of nervous activity, the reflex arc. These basic reflex units are the foundation for a functional neuromuscular mechanism. The random, symmetrical (two arms or two legs moving together) body movements of the infant likewise ensure a certain basic, functional level of increasing responsive and volitional behavior. Know-how, in this sense referring to patterns of movement and action—both overt and covert—requires attention and directed effort. Lawther (1968) writes: "The time factor, insofar as it involves the quantity-of-experience factor, is often overlooked. The normal preschool child seems to be vigorously active in physical play eight or more hours every day" (p. 23). It takes time for neuromuscular development to occur.

Continuous activity, particularly during toddlerhood and early childhood, is essential for an optimal rather than a marginal level of motor performance. This fact cannot be stressed too strongly, for it has been demonstrated that development of nerve tissue and its use are mutually enhancing. In order for the neuromuscular mechanism to become functional, it must be used, and use facilitates further development.

In order to understand where children between the ages of 2½ and 5 are on this movement continuum, it is necessary to study two parameters of development: physical growth and neuromuscular changes. Stewart's (1974) presentation of motor development during infancy is well worth concentrated study as a basis for understanding the neuromuscular foundations that have already been laid down by most children by this time. Her presentation of the stages in the development of upright posture show the initial difficulty the infant has in coming to terms with gravity. The work of Holle (1976) presents the details of some of the reasons for this difficulty,

Stability: controlling the body in an upright position. There is psychological security to be gained from successful practice at a low height before moving on to ones as tall as the child.

but neither discussion bears repetition here, since 2½-year-olds—unless classified as children with special needs—are posttoddlers, past the stages that these two authors treat so expertly.

Smith and Smith's (1972) classification of behavior into *stability, locomotion,* and *manipulation* does merit consideration.* Most of the neuromuscular action involved in stability is reflex in nature. The *stretch reflex,* for example, is mainly responsible for upright posture. The simplest of the spinal *sensory-motor* reflexes, the stretch reflex is a reflex arc involving only one sensory neuron and one motor neuron (a nerve cell supplying a muscle), which is activated when a muscle is stretched. *Sensory-motor* is a term used to indicate a relationship between incoming sensations and the resultant motor action. The children of this text are learning to cope with stability under varying environmental conditions that make new and different demands on their neuromuscular systems. For example, some 2½-year-olds do not have a true run (this involves a period of nonsupport), for they have not yet developed leg strength sufficient to propel the body into the air and/or equilibrium sufficient to maintain stability. The two are

*From K. V. Smith and W. M. Smith, *Perception and Motion: An Analysis of Space-Structured Behavior* (Philadelphia, PA: W. B. Saunders, 1972), p. 6.

Locomotion: a two-foot to landing-on-two-feet jump, very well executed by this 4-year-old.

related. Muscular responsiveness and strength are major components of stability, and stability is an underlying factor of locomotion.

Crawling and creeping are initial forms of locomotion. The alternation and opposition of arm and leg movement evidenced in these two activities is also demanded in climbing a ladder. Because the body may assume a different posture in climbing, the stability component changes. The author has seen infants, that is, nonwalkers, who could climb up a slide or a ladder with comparative ease. This is an excellent example of the practice of emerging skills. It is also good preliminary movement for the final act of walking and for the more mature skill of running.

Since the fine, manipulative motor acts are the last to mature neurologically, it is fitting to treat them separately, although the ability to pick something up—using thumb and finger in opposition—is dependent upon the ability to stabilize the body. There is a relationship between the two, and they develop concomitantly. Because writing is a necessary school skill and a fine motor act, educators have always been interested in its development and in activities that would facilitate it. They have not, however, provided for or supported to such a degree the development of stability and the gross motor skills of locomotion, and this is really what

Manipulation. Even this 3-year-old likes to kick.

early childhood is all about. Children of 2½ to 5 are actively, and very personally, involved in two major and related growth tasks—namely, seeing themselves as persons distinct from parents and/or siblings, and practicing being independent, making decisions that permit them to function as autonomous individuals. Control over stability and locomotion is a major factor in this sense of independence.

Bruner (1965) addresses this very succinctly when he says: ". . . the degree to which competence or mastery come to control behavior, to that degree the role of reinforcement wanes in shaping behavior" (p. 72). Nowhere is this development of control so important as in the control of the body—neuromuscular coordination and those motor acts of getting about in living and playing.

Physical Changes, Ages 2½ to 5

It is important to understand the two major changes of the body that come about with age and with use—namely, change in *size*, which may be

A 2-year-old's first day at school. Up . . .
. . . and over . . .
. . . by myself.

Search for autonomy. "Just two. I can balance and climb. Do I love it? Doesn't my face tell?"

termed *growth*, and change in *function*, which is termed *development*. The first represents increments or decrements of any part or organ of the body, and it is quantitative. The second reflects increased complexity of the systems of the body and has, therefore, a qualitative dimension. Systems, like the muscular or circulatory ones, do different things, perform different functions.

> *Growth is childhood's essential characteristic.*
> ROUSSEAU

Growth

There are three facts about growth that have a direct relationship to motor development and performance and therefore must be understood.

1. Growth does not take place at an even pace. There are spurts and periods of consolidation.
2. The period of most rapid growth is during the first six years.
3. Environmental influences are greatest during the periods of most rapid growth.

"Large-muscle activity is my way of life. I need lots of practice."

These, then, would seem to dictate the importance of the age span under consideration. There are three other aspects of growth that are important to understand.

Increased size. Children aged 2½ to 5 are still growing taller and larger, but the very rapid growth of the first two years, including that of the prenatal period, has begun to slow down. This is termed a period of consolidation of the growth pattern and may be seen as a time when children have to learn to use the increased length of their arms and legs and to control their weight in movement patterns. The 2½-year-old no longer knocks over his glass of milk, because his visual information coincides with his knowledge of the length of his arms.

Differential growth. The "baby" fat of the toddler is replaced by the leaner body of the more active child. The "string" around the wrist and the dimples of the hands disappear as activity utilizes the fat as a source of energy. Growth of the body now takes on this differential aspect, which is nowhere so well illustrated as in the growth of the head. The infant's head is approximately one-quarter of its total body length. But the growth of the head—which initially exerts such an antigravity problem—slows down, and total body growth becomes represented more and more by increased leg length. This differential growth pattern is exhibited throughout the entire body, but three examples—increased muscle mass, increased length of limb, and increased neural tissue—contribute substantially to improvement in motor performance.

Decreased size. Although this is an anatomical fact, it is not important to this age group. There may be decreased girth in the abdomen, for example, but this is more representative of differential growth, as mentioned before. Proportions do change during this time span, but they do not, on the whole, represent a decrease in size of a body part or system as they do during later ages, when there may be atrophy and/or decremental growth.

Implications. These three aspects of growth are a function of age but are influenced by activity, particularly by gross motor activity. The exchange of proportionally more muscle for fat means greater power to act, since muscles are the propelling force of the body, and fat represents dead weight. Longer length of limb means greater lever length over which the muscles can exert force. Increased neural growth, which is just about concluded during this period, represents, in part, the final aspects of brain growth. By 2½ children have reached one-half their adult height, and there is then a slow but steady decline in the rate of growth until puberty. Combine these factors of growth with what is known about growth in intelligence—namely, that about 50 percent is achieved by age 4—and perhaps the marked influence that environment can have on total functioning will be better understood.

Development

Concomitant changes in physical development result in changes in function, and nowhere is this so dramatically illustrated as in this presentation, which shows that skin, muscle, and nerve tissues originate from the same structure.

Patterns of Development

There is differentiation of function within the systems as well as between them. The muscular system, for example, has *striated* (or striped) muscles attached to the skeleton that function to effect movement, and smooth muscles—located for the most part in visceral walls and blood vessels whose function is the transport of body substances. There is also cardiac muscle and all these are involved in some way with activity, that is, demands are made upon them by vigorous activity. It is the development and use of the first which is the concern of this book but it bears repeating that the nutritional status and functioning of all three are affected by activity. Contributions of activity to the cardiovascular system at later ages is well documented, and as we begin to work more extensively with children with special needs, we see the reciprocal relationship between activity and improved functioning of most systems of the body. The focus here, however, is on neuromuscular functioning and facilitation, or making neural transmission easy.

Neuromuscular development of the body follows very specific principles: *cephalocaudal* (from head to tail) pattern, *proximal–distal* (from near to far) direction, *gross–fine* (from those muscles with a large to small innervation ratio) refinement. In essence, this means that those parts and systems nearest the head grow and develop first, and those furthest away, like the hands, mature in structure and function later.

Model of Development

The focus of this text is on gross movements as distinct from fine movements. This distinction is the result of the innervation ratio of motor neurons to muscle fibers. In the large muscles of the leg, for example, the ratio is 1 motor neuron to 150 fibers, which results in a large or gross movement. There is a ratio of 1 motor neuron to 3 muscle fibers in the eye, which permits more precise movement. Although there is some provision for throwing and catching, the major thrust is one of permitting these children to practice the emerging skills of total body assembly. Teeple

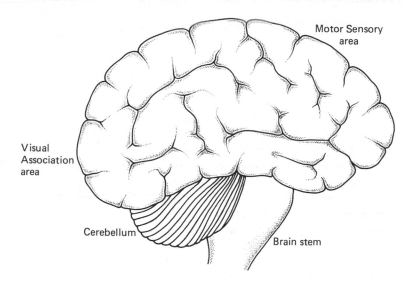

Birth of the Nervous System

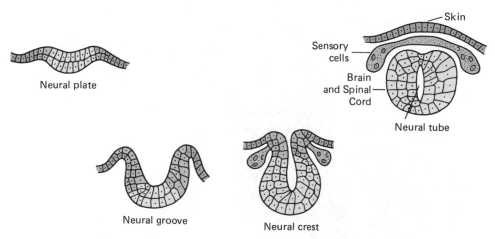

Example of growth and development of the brain.

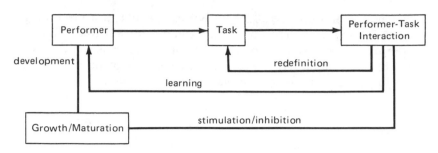

Relationships of dynamic components in skill acquisition. (From Janet Teeple, "Physical Growth and Maturation," in M. V. Ridenour et al. (Ed.), *Motor Development: Issues and Applications,* Princeton, NJ: Princeton Book Co., 1978, p. 5.)

(1978) offers a motor development model that expresses relationships of the dynamic components involved in skill acquisition:

In summary, it may be said that 2½- to 5-year-olds characteristically gain height and weight, lose fatty tissue, and develop muscle tissue and neuromuscular control. Thus we see that this is a period of human growth that is characterized by a reproportionment of the body more rapid and more dramatic in nature than at any other time. White's (1975) research

Changing dimensions. Two, three, and four.

indicates that these children are involved in a process of refinement of abilities rather than the discovery of new ones (p. 259). It is thus fitting to observe more closely what contributions strenuous, selected activity makes to the development of purposeful movement.

References

JEROME BRUNER, "The Act of Discovery." In Ira Gordon (Ed.), *Human Development: Readings in Research* (Glenview, IL: Scott, Foresman and Co., 1965).

BRITTA HOLLE, *Motor Development in Children, Normal and Retarded* (London: Blackwell Scientific Publications, 1976).

JOHN LAWTHER, *The Learning of Physical Skills* (Foundations of Physical Education series) (Englewood Cliffs, N.J.: Prentice-Hall, Inc., 1968).

MARY LOU STEWART, *The Process of Motor Co-ordination in the Human Infant* (College of Education Monograph Series) (Kalamazoo, MI: Western Michigan University, 1974).

JANET TEEPLE, "Physical Growth and Maturation." In Marcella V. Ridenour and others (Ed.), *Motor Development: Issues and Applications* (Princeton, N.J.: Princeton Book Co., 1978).

BURTON L. WHITE, *The First Three Years of Life* (Englewood Cliffs, N.J.: Prentice-Hall, Inc., 1975).

3

Neuromuscular Mechanism

Man is constantly enjoying stimulating
his vestibular apparatus and challenging his equilibrium,
pitting his skills against the earth's gravitational pull
*from the time he first lifts his head.**

A small boy enters the gymnasium, sees the springboard, runs directly toward it, jumps, performs a forward roll, and comes up running to repeat his movement sequence. How, one may ask, is such a young child able to perform such a highly skilled movement?

The performer has taken into account factors and properties of the environment external to the body: His vision tells him about the distance to the springboard and its height; his tactile sense informs him of the hard-

*From Jean A. Ayers, *Sensory Integration and Learning Disorders* (Los Angeles, CA.: Western Psychological Services, 1977).

21

Highly skilled movement. On the playground, the 3-year-old finds a wonderful piece of climbing apparatus to jump from.

ness of the gymnasium floor, the stiffness of the board, the softness of the protective mat; his auditory sense tells him about the speed at which he is running as his steps echo through the gym.

But knowledge of how his body reacts to these properties of the environment is also available to him through his internal senses. The *vestibular apparatus*, the sensory receptors located inside the inner ear, keeps the body informed of the position of the head and is sensitive to sudden changes in the direction of the body. It contributes to the cocontraction of muscular patterns for balance. Joint receptors monitor the position of body parts such as the upper and lower part of the leg and its relation to the trunk as the child moves through this sequence. *Muscle spindles* and *Golgi tendon organs* keep the brain informed of the state of contraction of the muscles.

His decision of how fast to run, when to jump, and how to roll is a cortical one; that is, it is under voluntary control. When the small boy wishes to change his running and jumping pattern, he has to "think" about it and formulate a new motor plan. According to Evarts (1973): "The highest brain functions are generally thought to be mediated in the cerebral cortex. In the control of muscles, however, the highest function may be served by the cerebellum, basal ganglion and the thalamus" (p. 96). The decisions involved are at the cortical level of control. Sensory information from all the senses, stimuli from both external and internal sources, are integrated with *kinesthetic* (the sense attributed to the knowledge of body position) memory of past experiences to produce a highly controlled, skilled movement.

Although it requires a basic knowledge of human anatomy and kinesiology to understand fully what is happening to our small boy, it is well worth the effort of attaining that knowledge to appreciate fully both what has been achieved and what can be expected in the future. In the next few pages, I present a simple description of this knowledge. Further references may be made to the books recommended at the conclusion of the chapter to help in understanding why children who are exposed to certain motor skills early in life tend to excel in the development of later skills.

Volitional Movement

The neuromuscular mechanism is a complex one that is often over-simplified. It is an intricate nerve–muscle network unit. Granit (1970) states:

> Coordinated movement is an extremely intricate and complicated phenomenon of bio-engineering, and modern man scarcely scratches the surface of movement potential. Motor acts such as walking which most of us take for granted are, in fact, a succession of motorically programmed flexor contractions with extensor inhibitions, followed by extensor contraction and flexor inhibition. This well-organized cooperation is dependent upon positive and negative feedback supplied by the powerful *stretch reflex* and *Golgi tendon organs*.

These aspects of the feedback mechanism are discussed in more detail in a subsequent part of this chapter.

Skilled movement is planned movement. There are three major steps involved in formulating a motor plan:

1. An appropriate cue is selected for the desired outcome. In the example given, the boy spotted the springboard and formulated a plan that would take him directly to it and that included a mental picture of the jump and the roll.
2. The information is integrated with past experience so that the child can decide and select the appropriate plan. His experience with running

and accelerating his speed, then slowing just as he made the jump in order to convert linear motion to vertical motion, provided a basis for judgments about speed, timing, and force needed for the succession of movements.

3. An effective motor pathway is developed that gives feedback information about the appropriateness of steps one, two, and three.

Central Nervous System

The nervous system is functionally organized into three specialized neuronal units: those that serve as *receptors*, others as *integrators*, and the *motor neurons*, whose function is to *activate* muscles and glands. When the nervous system is described according to location in the body, there is the *central nervous system* (CNS), which includes the brain and the spinal cord, and the *peripheral nervous system* (PNS), including the sensory and final motor neurons. It also includes the greater portion of the autonomic system, including the heart, lungs, and other involuntary organs.

Movement is dependent upon the ability of the body to select and receive sensations; to translate, code, and store information about the sensations; and to decide whether or not to respond to the information. Movement can be initiated in the brain without benefit of sensory stimulation. For example, a child may decide to run, not because she sees anything to run after, but as a conscious, overt act of volition. Or incoming sensory

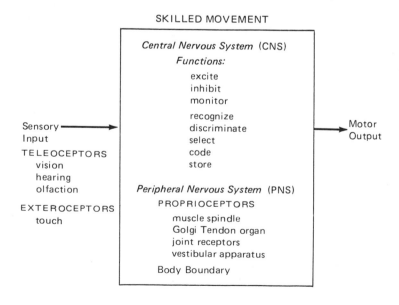

SKILLED MOVEMENT

Central Nervous System (CNS)

Functions:

excite
inhibit
monitor

recognize
discriminate
select
code
store

Sensory Input

TELEOCEPTORS
vision
hearing
olfaction

EXTEROCEPTORS
touch

Peripheral Nervous System (PNS)

PROPRIOCEPTORS
muscle spindle
Golgi Tendon organ
joint receptors
vestibular apparatus

Body Boundary

Motor Output

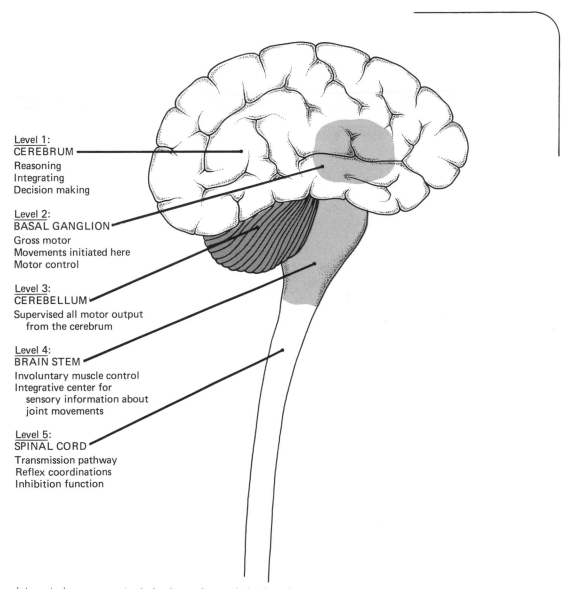

Level 1:
CEREBRUM
Reasoning
Integrating
Decision making

Level 2:
BASAL GANGLION
Gross motor
Movements initiated here
Motor control

Level 3:
CEREBELLUM
Supervised all motor output
    from the cerebrum

Level 4:
BRAIN STEM
Involuntary muscle control
Integrative center for
    sensory information about
    joint movements

Level 5:
SPINAL CORD
Transmission pathway
Reflex coordinations
Inhibition function

Integrated sensory-motor behavior and associative learning.

information from one of the senses—the eyes, for example—may stimulate action. The child may see a bright ball, and she wishes to grasp it. This decision may be followed by careful consideration in the prefrontal area (judgment) of the brain, where the whole or part of the movement plan may be initiated or inhibited. When a course of action is selected, as in running, the action is initiated by the motor cortex. Decision making is thus an integral part of motor planning, and of cognitive development.

Functions of the Nervous System
in Motor Control

Within the nervous system there are five levels of function that are important for an understanding of volitional and automated motor control and learning. These are interdependent and may represent similar or dissimilar functions. The overlapping of functions is one way of ensuring that motor performance will occur. (See figure on page 25.)

Level One: Cerebral Cortex

This level represents the highest—that is, the most volitional—level of motor control. Movement, particularly in the learning stage, may be initiated on command of the motor cortex, and it is believed that fine motor coordinations, such as putting pegs in a hole or writing, are controlled at this level. There are, however, at least four major functions of the cerebral cortex that are relevant to this study: (1) *reception* of sensory information from all senses of the body; (2) *integration* of this information with memories of past motor experiences in order to make decisions; (3) *formulation* of a motor plan (this function is the result of the combined activity of the entire cortex and represents what is called "volitional control"; it provides the basis for integrated behavior and associated learning); (4) *correction* of motor performance. Recurrent collateral fibers, which have the ability to produce recurrent *inhibition*, stabilize both the rate and the number of firing cells for a given movement. The motor act, whether a movement or an inhibition of a movement, is the result of an interpretation of the input. Neural *inhibition* is one of the most significant functions of the higher centers of the CNS.

CEREBRAL CORTEX

Integrator
decision maker

volitional
or sensory input ———————→   ————————→ motor output

Level Two: Basal Ganglion

Within the cerebral hemispheres are masses of neurons that are called the *basal ganglia*. These neurons form a network of *afferent* and *efferent* fibers that carry messages to and from the motor cortex and exercise control over movement by acting in both a facilitating and inhibitory capacity. Learned gross movements are initiated at this level. So the small boy in our illustration does not have to "think" about running or jumping, because these gross movements now represent *automated* behavior. The major role of the basal ganglion is to generate slow movements.

BASAL GANGLION

Initiator
of
gross movements
sensory input ———————▶ slow ———————▶ motor output

Level Three: Cerebellum

The *cerebellum* (little brain) serves as the *integrative* center for postural adjustments (standing upright), locomotive activity (speed of running), and reflex activity (stretch reflex). It has been compared to a switchboard that keeps both the higher and lower centers of the nervous system coordinated. There are three functions of the *cerebellum* that are of significance to this text:

1. Service as a *feedback* loop during motor activity concerning the body in space. If, for example, the young boy begins to lean too far forward in his running pattern, the cerebellum provides instant feedback to the higher centers—the *basal ganglion* and the *motor cortex*—and to the lower center—the *brain stem*—to correct the body position. With practice, this feedback mechanism becomes very precise in the information it transmits, so the movement patterns become more refined and mature in appearance.
2. *Integration* of information from the vestibular mechanism with visual and proprioceptive data. The boy is able to perform a forward roll because his nervous system is capable of controlling his stability in a turning motion that involves a complicated combination of *excitation* and *inhibition* of reflex activity.
3. *Exertion* of temporal control over the contraction of the *prime mover (agonist)* and the *antagonist*. The running movement of the small boy is a constant interplay of action of the *flexors* and *extensors* of the legs and hips. Thus the major role of the *cerebellum* may be considered receiving information from the *motor cortex* and from the sense organs, and monitoring and mediating information from other centers of the nervous system. The *Purkinje cells*, which comprise the middle layer of the cerebellum, are engaged in the control of even the smallest measurable motor effect.

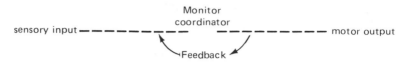

CEREBELLUM

Monitor
coordinator
sensory input — — — — — — — — — — — — — — motor output

Feedback

Level Four: Brain Stem

A major function of the *brain stem* is the control of involuntary motor movements such as those involved in maintaining equilibrium. It does, in fact, serve as an integrative center for combining and coordinating all sensory-motor information. It is at this level of neurological functioning that sensory information about joint movements and positions and information from the *vestibular mechanism* about the motion and position of the head are integrated. So, with practice, the small boy has educated his body to tuck the head and assume a tightly curled position for the forward roll. And the *brain stem* serves in a feedback capacity to keep the brain apprised of the tightness of the curl, the tucking of the head, and the forward, rolling motion of the boy's body.

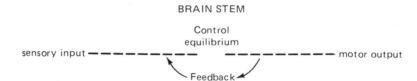

BRAIN STEM

Control
equilibrium
sensory input — — — — — — — — — — — — — — motor output

Feedback

Level Five: Spinal Cord

The *spinal cord* is the major pathway for the transmission of sensory information to muscles (and glands). Reflex coordinations—such as the stretch reflex, which is mainly responsible for upright posture—occur at this level. Both facilitory and inhibitory mechanisms are utilized to effect and achieve muscle control at this level. Collateral impulses stimulate inhibitory neurons, which control the antagonist. When the small boy was "learning" to run, what was really happening to his body was that the reciprocal relationship between *agonist* and *antagonist* was being smoothed out, so the running became progressively faster and stronger.

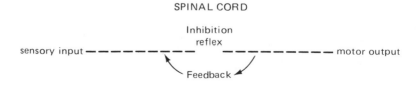

SPINAL CORD

Inhibition
reflex
sensory input — — — — — — — — — — — — — — motor output

Feedback

Neuronal Growth

Edington and Edgerton (1976) state:

> At birth, most neurons are already formed although not fully developed. Axons and dendrites proliferate rapidly in the first months of life. These changes coincide with apparent improvement in muscular coordination. How these neural maturation patterns relate to coordinated movement in young girls and boys is yet to be determined. (p. 237)

However, it is known that myelinization is necessary for a nerve impulse to travel from a nerve center along to fiber to a part or parts of the nervous system. The spinal cord, where reflex actions take place, is myelinated at birth, but the newborn has no cortical control over lower centers of the brain because myelinization has not yet occurred. A strong connection is, therefore, shown between the development of myelin and motor development. Certain coordinations, such as creeping and walking, must await the development of myelin sheaths along the appropriate nerves and spinal tracts. Myelinization of some axons is responsive to use, but according to Edington and Edgerton (1976), the effects of postnatal physical activity are not yet known. The intent of physical activity during early childhood is to optimize opportunity for utilizing the motor skills that children have achieved at whatever level of development they happen to be.

The following conclusions can be drawn from the material presented in this section:

1. Motor systems appear to function under several levels of control.
2. The higher levels exercise control over the lower ones, but much orderly, integrated motor behavior occurs without interference from the higher levels.
3. Higher levels can modify lower levels at will.
4. By a process that is little understood, movement patterns come to be controlled by lower centers as they become well learned and can be performed with little conscious awareness.

The three basic aspects of coordinated movement that must be fulfilled by the CNS are (1) selection of the appropriate muscle (spatial control); (2) muscle activation or inactivation, which must occur at the appropriate time (temporal control); and (3) gradation of the degree of muscle inactivation (quantitative control) (Evarts, 1971).

Harrison (1975) says:

In the short term, what is important is whether the subject can compose a movement program which is adequate for the task he is facing. In the long term, what may be important is whether he has learned anything which he can generalize to new tasks (p. 25).*

Peripheral Nervous System

In order to perform efficiently, effectively, or expressively, the body must monitor its own movements by knowing the relative positions of its different parts and by being able to maintain a particular orientation toward gravity. The contributions the visual and auditory senses make to motor learning have been studied quite extensively. These senses depend almost exclusively upon stimuli received from outside the body, although each contributes in a very specific way to the control of equilibrium via internal feedback. The eyes monitor the position of the head, and the *labyrinthine* senses of the ear keep the body in a proper position relative to gravity.

As may be seen from the figure on page 24, there are various types of

There are many ways to hang upside-down. Note that toes as well as hands grip tightly.

*Ann Harrison, "Components of Neuromuscular Control," in Kenneth Holt, *Movement and Child Development*, Clinics in Developmental Medicine No. 55 (Philadelphia: J. B. Lippincott, 1975).

body receptors that aid in the awareness of total body orientation to space. Cutaneous and muscle receptors, located in the soles of the feet and the buttocks, are sensitive to tactile pressure and inform people whether they are sitting or standing. Other types of sense organs, *muscle spindles*, are specialized muscle fibers interspersed in all the skeletal muscles of the body. Each spindle has a noncontractile center that contains the receptor endings. Muscle spindles initiate the stretch reflex. The *Golgi tendon organ* is the sensory receptor that is responsible for detection of tension on a tendon and the extent of muscle contraction. It is located in the tendon near the ends of the muscle fibers and functions as an inhibitory mechanism. *Joint receptors*, sometimes called *kinesthetic receptors*, are found in joints throughout the body. They are stimulated when the bones that come together at a joint are moved in any direction.

The receptors for the *labyrinthine* senses are located in nonauditory portions of the cochlear canals of the inner ear and are referred to as the *vestibular apparatus*. This part of the structure is made up of five distinct parts: three *semicircular canals*, the *utricle*, and the *saccule*. Although there is some projection of nervous energy to the cortex, most vestibular input is responsible for reflexive postural adjustments and would thus be classified as nonvolitional movement.

Being upside-down is quite a different sensation from being right side up.

The major feedback mechanisms of the body are the *proprioceptors*, which include those complex sensory receptors of the muscle spindles, the Golgi tendon organs, the joint receptors, and the vestibular apparatus. Receiving information from the muscles, tendons, joints, and vestibular apparatus, the proprioceptors make it possible for the body to monitor its own movements throughout all motor sequences. It is also worth noting that proprioceptive stimulation induces the most widespread cortical activation of any sense modality.

One of the goals of motor learning is to reduce movements that are nonessential to skilled performance. Once the image of a task is clear and a motor plan formulated, practice becomes extremely important. Young children need time to practice emerging skills, for they are at the stage of learning when their neuromuscular maturation is approximating its zenith. The concurrence of neuromuscular maturation and interest in large muscle activity makes learning relatively easy, and educators should capitalize on this fact.

Motor planning: skilled performance of a 3-year-old. The task (to climb to the top) is clear. The motor plan has been formulated—now to practice.

Muscular System

In order to understand the motor aspect of the neuromuscular mechanism more thoroughly, a basic knowledge of the function, arrangement, and structure of muscles and tendons and of their *proprioceptive* mechanisms is necessary. This knowledge, coupled with the preceding discussion of the sensory system, provides a basis for understanding how their actions are integrated to achieve purposeful movement.

Arrangement

Movement is dependent on the reciprocal relationship of paired muscles that direct and control motor responses. These pairs involve articulation of the joints of the body. Movement is, therefore, an outcome of the coordinated action of these pairs. With the action of the *prime mover*, also called the *agonist* and responsible for the desired movement, the movement of the *antagonist* must be inhibited. It is partly the speed with which this latter event occurs that determines the speed of contraction of the prime mover.

Excitation and Inhibition

Muscles contract or shorten because of a stream of impulses that reach them through the neural *synapses* or junctions. A nerve fiber can innervate several muscle fibers, but ordinarily, a muscle fiber receives only one nerve fiber. The chemical reaction that occurs between the motor neuron and the resting muscle fiber generates excitatory postsynaptic potentials, or EPSPs. This event is what is termed *excitation*, and the result is usually movement of some kind.

But not all neuronal activity results in excitation; responses can be prevented or inhibited. This is a fairly simple phenomenon. The generation at the synapses is of *inhibitory* postsynaptic potentials, or IPSPs.

> Whenever an inhibitory neuron delivers its impulses at the synapse, it creates in the recipient neuron an event whose electrical sign is opposite to that of an excitatory neuron. IPSPs oppose EPSPs; when an IPSP occurs along with an EPSP, the two cancel out and the recipient neuron shows no response at all. (Galambos, 1962, p. 440).

The development of these excitatory and inhibitory mechanisms is particularly rapid during early childhood; it is, in fact, a critical period for their development. Edington and Edgerton (1976) state that in the formative process of axonal connection to skeletal muscles, motor activities seem to be the most critical. Development of muscular, ligamentous, and tendinous growth occurs concurrently with exercise, but it is important to remember that it is the neuromuscular development that makes this possible. And it is the demands of activities such as climbing, hanging, and swinging, the major concerns of a later part of this book, that facilitate neuromuscular development.

Kinds of Muscles

Striated muscles, those muscles that are attached to the skeleton, are responsible for moving the various parts of the body. They also prevent movement, as in the postural relationships with gravity; that is, they allow the body to remain upright and resist the pull of gravity.

A further distinction of striated muscles is based on their function: *extrafusal* and *intrafusal*. There are two kinds of *extrafusal muscles:* The red, which join adjacent limbs, are slow in firing, are capable of holding a contraction, and do not fatigue easily. These function primarily to maintain posture. The red color that characterizes them is due to a high concentration of myoglobin, an oxygen-storing compound similar to hemoglobin in the blood. The *white* type is capable of faster contraction, fires faster, and extends over two or more joints, which means that they are not so deep-seated as the red. Both of these have mononeural innervation patterns.

Intrafusal muscles are the muscle fibers containing the stretch receptors. These specialized neuromuscular spindles measure the length and tension of the muscle and thus serve as an integral part of the feedback mechanism described earlier. The muscle spindles are, in fact, the most elaborate sensory structures in the body outside of the eyes and ears. They function at a subconscious level in what may be termed a subservient role. The stimulus that excites a muscle spindle is the stretching of the specialized sensory region.

Terminals of the muscle spindle afferents end on the intrafusal fiber. Spindles are responsive to changes in joint position, velocity of movement, and stretching of the involved muscle. They register total and segmental body positions and velocity of limb movement as well as muscular excitation. There are dynamic fibers that measure the velocity of stretching as well.

Neuron Ratio

Muscles also differ in contraction speed because of the neuron ratio. Each motor nerve fiber divides into terminals whose end plates are distributed onto a considerable number of muscle fibers. This is called a *motor unit*. The smaller the ratio of neurons to muscle fibers, the greater the speed of movement and the more discrete the movement. This fact accounts in part for Holt's (1975) distinction of parameters of movement between gross-postural and fine-visual. Thus the importance and dominance of vision as a responsive sense modality can be seen.

It is the science of motor psychophysics that has begun to explain the reciprocal problem of the relation between a conscious effort of will and the resulting motor patterns. Learning a new motor skill or improving an old one involves intent or a conscious effort. It is the thesis of this text that planned physical activity can and does contribute to increasingly more complicated motor patterns as children engage in purposeful movement.

References

DEE W. EDINGTON & V. R. EDGERTON, *The Biology of Physical Exercise* (Boston, MA: Houghton Mifflin, 1976).

EDWARD V. EVARTS, *Brain Mechanisms in Movement* (San Francisco, CA: Scientific American Offprints, W. H. Freeman and Co., July 1973) 229, no. 1, 96–103.

ROBERT GALAMBOS, *Nerves and Muscles; An Introduction to Biophysics* (Garden City, NY: Doubleday & Company, Inc., 1962).

RAGNAR GRANIT, *The Basis of Motor Control* (New York: Academic Press, 1970).

ANN HARRISON, "Components of Neuromuscular Control," in Kenneth Holt, (Ed.), *Movement and Child Development* (Philadelphia: J. B. Lippincott Co., 1975).

4

Contributions
of Active Play
to Cognitive
Development

*. . . a "person" subsumes intellectual, psychological and psychomotor elements
in his development and both of these are centrally involved
in experience and awareness of the world.** *

In what ways does an activity experience in the gymnasium, playground,
or backyard meet the intellectual needs of children 2½ to 5 years of age?
Rather than attempting to discuss or demonstrate a relationship between
motor skills and intellectual development, it seems more prudent to look at
possible contributions this particular kind of an environment can or does
make to cognitive development. It is evident from working with young
children that there are at least four contributions:

*From D.N. Aspin, *Kinds of Knowledge, Physical Education and the Curriculum* (London:
Lepus Books, 1977, and *Journal of Human Movement Studies*, 3, 1977, p. 35).

Know-how. Almost every child likes to swing or climb ropes. And at 4, their hands are scarcely large enough to have a firm grip.

1. It develops a vocabulary of movement terms.
2. It gives them many opportunities to make decisions.
3. It permits them or, perhaps more strongly, it challenges them to pose and to solve problems of space, time, force, and relationships.
4. It holds them responsible for the consequences of their actions.

"Know-how," says Aspin (1977), "is . . . some kind of continuum . . . [referring] to patterns of movement and overt and covert action that at some stage requires the bringing to bear of attention and directed effort" (p. 35).* An example of this is the jump, which is a whole series of moves that involve the application of judgment, and it is with "the development of judgment and understanding . . . that education and educators are concerned" (p. 35). The development of skilled action is an integral part of the gymnasium experience, and this development is predicated on increased perceptual-motor discrimination and the opportunity to make judgments. Every motor act the child makes involves the exercise of judgment and

*From D. N. Aspin, *Kinds of Knowledge, Physical Education, and the Curriculum* (*Journal of Human Movement Studies*, 3, 1977, pp. 21–37).

discrimination of some kind or degree. Motor and ideational processes are functions of separate sensory areas of the cerebral cortex, but the two are linked by the degree of conscious control exerted in the process of learning a skill, or when activities like gymnastics stress volitional control of movement. The child who runs under a ladder has to discern its height and decide whether it is necessary to duck or not. The child who jumps from the springboard controls his or her body so a decision to roll can follow the jump if decided upon.

Action Vocabulary

What is also important is that the children are personally involved with the development of an action vocabulary. They are running instead of just learning to say the word. They are jumping rather than learning to spell it. In fact, many verbs of action can be explored and discovered in the gymnasium. These children are motorically oriented, and this aspect of education—namely, strengthening the personal involvement of the learner by letting him or her act on the environment—has great merit. These children are *actively* exploring and developing knowledge about all the exciting action words so vital to their developing ability to communicate.

Most teachers know that language helps in learning to reason, to think, and to form relationships. Thinking is a learnable skill, and problem solving, in which these children are involved, is an important factor in thinking.

Decision Making

Secondly, these activities in the gymnasium give children opportunities to make decisions; the freedom to make decisions is part of exercising responsibility. The ability to make decisions depends upon the ability to perceive alternatives and options. The range of options for action, and hence for decision making, is almost limitless; but it is restricted by the teacher's judicious selection of those activities thought to be at the children's developmental level. Freedom to select or to reject, then, is left to the individual child. Both the process of selecting or deciding and the product of the act are of extreme importance. Piaget (1951) calls this "growth through functioning." In his view, intelligence develops from an internalization of adaptive action upon the environment, which he terms *mental digestion*.

The decision-making process is also consistent with the current em-

Action vocabulary. "So many things to do the first day. I wonder what I'll do first—climb, balance, or jump."

phasis on movement education. Children are encouraged to develop their own motor plan of action that represents their ability to cope with the environment. Some young children, when approaching new equipment or the entire gymnasium for the first time, are "watchers." They learn, prior to participating directly by themselves, to watch what other children do by observing their peers in action. This period of observation may take place from the security of a teacher's lap, but it is to be respected. When the child is ready, he or she will make the first decision: to participate with more than just the eyes. It is important for us to remember that children of this age have just learned to trust the information they receive through vision, and they may need practice in making judgments based on this sense modality alone.

Equipment that will move, like rings and ropes, usually is attractive to most children from the start, and when they enter the gym, they make a beeline for it. The decision process is in action. They must then decide what to do on it, how to use it. A single rope hanging from the ceiling has many uses. Some children tuck their knees up to their chests and just hang. Some swing gently to and fro. Others keep their feet in contact with the

A watcher. This onlooker is very much involved in watching her peers slide. There are many opportunities to learn from watching.

floor and turn gently in a circle. Some ask to be lifted on and pushed. These are intellectual and emotional decisions. Still other children are actively experimenting with all the ways the rings can be used.

And then there was 5-year-old Danny. He always headed for a rope that he proceeded to climb to the very top. Four or five times in succession, he made the top of the rope before he headed off for another piece of apparatus. Who taught him to climb? Who knows? For he said that he had always known. He was the only one in a group of twenty with enough arm strength and "know-how" to get to the top.

Another day there was a game called "splat":

A bench had been set up near the ropes, so the children could launch themselves into a good swing. There was a mat under the ropes that made falling a skill to be developed. Very soon all of the children using the ropes were imitating the leader, who would launch himself and swing with glee and a certain sense of abandon before dropping with a "splat" to the mat.

This activity was great fun for all who participated, and the careful attention of the adult present served to exercise the necessary restraint so the activity kept well within safety bounds. It did result in forward rolls, drop-and-run tactics, and quite a variety of self-initiated tasks.

Decision number three involves how long to stay on the selected apparatus. This, too, is the child's decision, for most of the time there is no need to take turns, although they soon learn to do this without being asked. When there is equipment enough, taking turns is not a problem, but awaiting one's turn is a decision in itself. Most children decide very quickly not to stand in line, but the duration of the stay is interesting to observe and tells us quite a lot about individual children.

Melissa, age 20 months, spent twenty minutes learning to climb a ladder that had a board on it, thus making its center into a slide. She had never seen a ladder before, so this was a new challenge. The details of her learning to cope with the ladder are referred to later. She decided how high to go and when to try to turn around. Because of the differing visual field, turning around presents children with a problem. When she did turn and slide down, we who watched could almost hear her say, "That's enough"; and off she went to the ropes, where she took only one try at hanging, then left to attempt activities on the springboard. Her first "jump" was the characteristic "step

Problem solving. Dylan climbs up and over while others go through and under.

down" of that age. But in five or six minutes she was jumping off from her two feet and landing on two feet, a mature jump for a child of 20 months.

It would have been possible to calculate the number of overt decisions she made, but we shall never know of the things she rejected in this very important process. Cropley (1967) posits the notion that the greater the participation of the child in his or her own learning, the more likely it is that a divergent thinker or creative individual will emerge.

Problem Solving

Dewey, et al. (1970) stressed the importance of giving children the opportunity to grow intellectually through problem solving, because the process of learning, as well as the products, is important. Children who can use language to "speak in their heads" probably approach problem solving differently from those who are still thinking out loud or who have not formulated a very large action vocabulary. As selected children are observed, it is possible to discern what problems they have prepared and posed for themselves and to distinguish their way of solving them. Both the posing and solving of problems are integral parts of decision making, for once again, these involve being able to visualize alternatives and options. At this level of physical and intellectual functioning, there are no right or wrong answers unless there is a question of safety. At this point, the teacher has to intercede. The important factor is the freedom to pose problems, to seek solutions, and, finally, to live with the consequences. Parenthetically, it is interesting to follow one child and watch him or her wrap up a problem as Melissa did and then go on to something else. In Piagetian terms, this child has assimilated the reality of the environment and has experienced "growth through functioning."

But what, you may well ask, of the child with special, observable needs who does not eat of the smorgasbord of activities? Aaron, at 4½, was just such a child:

> His conversation was carried on at an adult level, and he was a precocious violinist. But he didn't like to climb or jump, and his

Puzzlement. What to do with the equipment today? Children are perfectly capable of setting some of the small equipment up in unique ways.

The outcome? Hurdles this 4-year-old clears with surprising form. These 4 x 4 x 12-inch pieces of wood, painted in different designs and colors and supporting a wand or broomstick, serve many functions. The hurdle itself becomes the instrument for learning.

running was not easy. So we arranged to play with him on an individual basis, one on one. Piggyback, tossing, chasing—all the fun things most children do with attentive, loving parents who understand the physical needs of a developing child. When some of his physical skills were on a par with those of his peers, he began to participate. This seemed to be an interesting case of intellectual astuteness coupled with fear of failure, retarded motor development, delayed experiences, and/or fear of activity in general.

The problems children pose and the decisions they make are intricately involved with the quantitative and comparative dimensions of space, time, and force, which, again, is consistent with the current emphasis on movement education. Going up and down a ladder provides experiences with height, plus the differing visual field involved in being at the top and turning around. Children's conception of space involves the relations of proximity, separation, and perspective. The concept of far-to-near is encountered as they approach the springboard. Balancing on a beam not only provides experience in the width of an object, which may force the child to decide whether to walk or crawl; it also involves separateness and perspective.

Balance. Razif, age 3, demonstrates the precision of a tightrope walker as he extends his hands and grips with his toes.

Devon, age 2½, slowly slides her feet across the balance beam. She does this back and forth several times. Next she begins to take actual steps, very slowly and carefully. She leaves the balance beam area to try out another piece of equipment but soon returns. She walks across the beam again, a little faster, spreading out her arms in balancing fashion. The observing teacher was not certain whether Devon had assumed this position in order to counteract unsteadiness or because she saw the girl who preceded her do it, but it did give the teacher the opportunity to verbalize a body concept: "You put your arms out so you wouldn't fall, didn't you?"

Climbing in a box or sitting under a ladder not only gives an estimate of space but helps children to determine how small they can make their bodies.

Crawling under or through space is accomplished with all the squeezing, twisting, and wriggling that accompanies such exploration:

Jon, age 3, crawls through the tunnel several times. He crawls through and runs around the tube, entering at the same end each time. Now

Space. "Tires make such good spaces to crawl through. Now, can I go head-first? I'll try."

Jon stops in the middle of the tunnel, explores the interior visually, looks at both openings. He then crawls through but this time reenters the tube at the end he just quitted.

Experiences like this promote an awareness of the body and how it moves, and an awareness of position in space and of the relationships of the body to surrounding environment. The characteristics of time, from the acceleration of the run to its full stop, become part of the world of action as well. If ever there was any personalized learning, it is right here in the gymnasium, where each child determines what he or she is ready to learn and to integrate with former learning and therefore sets the stage for the next level of development. Erikson (1963), addressing the contributions of the environment to learning, states: "Take [the force of] gravity . . . to jump or climb adds unused dimensions of the awareness of our body" (p. 206). Gravity is a constant environmental factor, and learning to cope with it is a major problem for all young children. First learning to hold the head up and then learning to sit, stand, and walk demands strength of the body adequate to counteract gravitational pull. Throwing a ball; cushioning a

Responsibility for consequences. Halfway up is far enough for Ayaka, age 3. Note the firm grip of her left hand; she's safe.

jump by bending knees, ankles, and hips; keeping the body round in a roll are ways of coping with the force of gravity.

Responsibility for Consequences

Being responsible for consequences is a final step in the decision process. Left on their own in this relatively safe environment, children are competent decision makers. For example, most children will climb only as high as they feel capable of ascending *and* descending. Of course, children who are constantly being put up on something and then taken down are postponing having to reckon with the consequences of their own action. Part of learning the consequences is being held actively responsible for *making* them. Children act on their environment in such a way as to be the cause of their own consequences, and they must be helped to see this. When they have to find their own way down, they are being held responsible. This action does not make timid children. It tends, rather, to produce children who can cope realistically with their own abilities.

Mastery means getting safely to the top.

I observed a 3½-year-old twin girl climb a set of stall bars (horizontal bars attached to the wall), launch herself on a swinging rope, and slide to the floor. She repeated this several times, climbing higher on the wall with each trial. Her head came near the bars with the swing but never did hit; even if it had, I doubt that it would have hurt much, for young children are such flyweights that the force of movement is often very small. Her next step was to "teach" this act to her twin brother, who, like her, began at the bottom and worked his way up.

The gymnasium is such a wonderful place to try out all these activities, because the child seldom loses face as a result of his or her actions. Other children are too busy to bother, and it is trying something that really matters. Piaget (1951), in reference to "Mastery Play," sums it all up: "This activity is no longer an effort to learn, it is only a happy display of known actions" (p. 113). We are, in fact, practicing what Pestalozzi, Froebel, Montessori, and A.S. Neil advocated (Castle, 1970) when we set up an environment that cultivates the child's understanding of self and world by independent, discriminating, and self-imposed activity. The writing of Bloom, Krathwoll, and Masia (1971) also has relevance here. Motor activity is, for most children, the *raison d'être*. They have a vital "interest in," "feel positively" about, and "avidly seek" large muscle activity. They go out of their way to express a liking for physical activity.

A 3-year-old told the teacher that unless the rings were taken down for him to use, he wanted to go home.

Because children are willing to attend (affective domain), particularly in the gymnasium, they will learn (cognitive domain). Children learn best through a combination of modeling, active involvement, and the joy of repetition. We will, as Gordon (1971) says: "design programs which emphasize their own activity, their own desire for growth, their own push to inquire, their own search for mastery" (p. 25).

References

BENJAMIN BLOOM, DAVID KRATHWOLL, and BERTRAM MASIA, *Taxonomy of Educational Objectives; Book 2, Affective Domain* (London: Longman Group, Ltd., 1971).

E. B. CASTLE, *The Teacher* (New York: Oxford University Press, 1970).

A. J. CROPLEY, *Creativity* (New York: Humanities Press, 1967).

JOHN DEWEY and others, *Creative Intelligence* (New York: Octagon Books, 1970).

ERIK ERIKSON, *Childhood and Society* (Rev. ed.) (New York: Norton, 1963).

IRA GORDON, "On Early Learning: The Modifiability of Human Potential," (Washington, D.C.: Association for Supervision and Curriculum Development, NEA, 1971).

JEAN PIAGET, "Mastery Play." In J. S. Bruner and others (Eds.), *Play* (New York: Penguin, 1951).

Contributions
of Active Play
to Psychological
Development

*Among these needs, five seem to be of particular significance
if children are to have an environment that is stimulating
for their personal growth. Acceptance. Achievement. Participation. Expressing feelings.
Guidance toward self-discipline. Their importance must not be underestimated,
for if they are ignored, the children will not be emotionally free to learn.* *

How children *feel* about movement may be more important than what they *know* about movement. In general, most children prefer moving to sitting or staying still, for moving "feels" good. So the affective domain as well as the psychomotor and cognitive domains must be considered. Besides meeting some of the needs just delineated, there are at least six ways in which purposeful physical activity in the gymnasium or playground contributes to psychological development:

*From Gladys Gardner Jenkins, *Helping Children Reach Their Potential* (Glenview, IL.: Scott, Foresman and Company, 1961), p. 11.

1. It enhances the concept of the self-image.
2. It helps to develop a sense of competence.
3. It reduces the stress of anticipation of success or failure.
4. It increases kinesthetic awareness, moving for the sheer good feeling of it.
5. It enhances a feeling of confidence.
6. It provides a positive setting for the development of self-knowledge.

Self-Image

If a playful atmosphere has been conscientiously and consistently provided, the children feel free to explore, manipulate, and discover; thus they tend to develop as self-initiating individuals. They develop as children who "can do" rather than as children who say "I can't do that" or "I don't want to do this." The sense of "let me do it" is very strong at age 2½, and the playful atmosphere tends to preserve rather than destroy it. Learning situations are provided in which the value of the experience in itself is

The "I can do" child. Sometimes it takes the whole body to hang on. Bare feet give added security and make it possible for David to get up on the uneven bars by himself.

acknowledged, instead of being regarded as preparation for something later on in life. They may, however, have a strong effect on molding the attitudes and performance abilities of these children later in life.

The predominance of gross motor abilities at this age makes it vital that a positive feeling about moving be encouraged and be satisfying if it is to persist. The acquisition of language and the development of the fine motor skills of writing tend to be provided for and rewarded in our society because of their positive relationship to academic success, as stated previously, but the foundations of self-esteem are laid down as the child develops the gross motor skills that precede development of fine ones. Baker (1966) says:

> In using his large muscles the child is easy and comfortable and free of the strain which comes when he uses his fine muscles. Through his motor accomplishments he is laying part of the basic pattern of self-confidence he needs. (p. 9)

How a child feels about moving determines to a large extent how he or she does move, whether freely and happily or with restraint and grudgingly. That these early childhood experiences have great potency is quite beyond doubt; so is the fact that their consequences are often long lasting and may be very difficult to alter. Phenix (1977) says: "It is important that the young learn to accept and enjoy their own feelings and to trust the messages they convey. To do so is the only basis for fostering a life with direct and unquestionable satisfactions" (p. 63). Feeling values constitute the basis for the sense of immediate worth in existence. They express present enjoyment of the quality of life.

There are both obvious and subtle forces at work that mitigate against children—especially little girls—moving freely and, hence, moving well and having a good feeling about it. Sex-appropriate behavior is well established during these preschool years, but fortunately, some of these attitudes and practices are changing as the line of demarcation between the physical performance of girls and boys at this age becomes eradicated. We know that attitudes and behaviors, both overt and covert, of adults provide children with critical messages about what is valued, what they may and may not do. The young child's experiences in the gymnasium with trained physical education teachers clearly stresses non-sex-differentiated expectations. In the typical classroom situation, however, teachers may, without awareness or intent, subtly reinforce children's conformity in perpetuation of traditional sex roles. For example, teachers may actually be socializing children into a role that demands passive, docile, conforming behavior (a rather traditional female role), to which girls may accommodate, whereas boys may experience role conflict. Since there are no demonstrations or explanations of skills, or ways in which the apparatus may be used, and since much of the apparatus is different from anything the children are likely to have seen before, there is little opportunity for anything but *child-appropriate* behavior to emerge. Boys are often observed to do more running than girls, but this is consistent with what is known about neuromuscular development of boys and not because they are "expected" to be more active than girls. The gymnasium setting is most appropriate for what Sprung (1975) suggests as a goal for nonsexist education—namely, to involve girls as well as boys in *active* play.

Competence

White (1966) believes that there is a drive for competence that stands on a par with the other basic drives such as hunger and love, to which so much attention has been given. It is the author's belief that the development of a sense of competence outweighs all other contributions that a program of physical activity may have for children of this age. In no other place—not on the playground nor in the backyard—are children exposed and invited to try so many daring activities, and nowhere is there greater opportunity for success. Not only do the children become confident and competent in a

Child-appropriate behavior. A bar for chinning or turning, with holes in the supports to accommodate children of different heights, can be made at home, as this one was.

Both competent and confident at 2½ years old.

wide variety of physical skills, but their ability to make decisions can be respected, trusted, and cherished. In fact, one of the major expectations is that the children will act in a competent, responsible way, and they usually do. The intent is not to develop star Olympic athletes. Rather, it is to foster happy, competent 2½ to 5-year-olds.

Within this atmosphere of trust and respect, the children feel free to try many new activities. Pringle (1975) identifies a need for new experiences as a basis for emotional growth. Certainly, if adults can respect and trust these young children, the likelihood of their trying new experiences will be greater, and the chance that they will develop good feelings about themselves and others is very great. Competence may not be synonymous with success, but it certainly is one of its major components and, without doubt, is the most likely psychological component to generate success.

Lack of Frustration

One of the major points made by Sylva, Bruner, and Genova (1976) is that with the playful experience, "there was a temporary moratorium on frustration" (p. 244). This is a very important point, since physical restraint, either imposed by others or by the developmental inability to do something, is the single most frustrating experience for many young children. The child who can't open a drawer is likely to kick it; the child who cannot take the lid off a box, to throw it. At this point in their intellectual development, they are unable to comprehend their lack of success, and no amount of explaining will help. Physical aggression is the most spontaneous form of coping response to failure. So frustration is a very real experience of childhood. And it often stands in the way of alternative solutions or actions.

Between the ages of 2½ and 5, because of the sequence of neuromuscular development, activities demanding fine muscular coordination are likely to be more frustrating than those making demands on gross motor mechanisms. It follows therefore that not only is there less frustration and fear of failure in a playful atmosphere, but also that most activities in a playful atmosphere are gross motor in nature, making it an experience most likely to imbue a sense of success, competence, and enjoyment. These gross motor activities present the opportunity for a nursery school that has a new commitment. Indoor activities in small spaces, particularly in the winter, impose a sense of restraint on children to whom being still is anathema. They will be quiet after large muscle activity, for they are like small, playful animals who seek rest and recovery after an unstinted output of energy. One nursery school teacher reports that the children not only sleep better on the days they come to the gymnasium, but they also eat better and are generally calmer for the remainder of the day.

> David, age 4, enters the gymnasium with a burst of energy not unlike that of a rocket being launched. Instead of heading for a particular piece of equipment as most of the other children do, he sets up his own quarter-mile track around the periphery of the gym. Round and round he goes with sudden bursts of speed when space permits but never a stop to catch his breath. Fifteen, twenty, twenty-five minutes later, and he is still running. To run seems to be his highest priority for the day. And for the next, and the next.

The lack of frustration may have greater and more potent ramifications for little boys than for little girls, whatever the cause. Sex differences in motor performance are reported consistently in the research literature, with boys demonstrating superior skill in gross motor activities like running, jumping, and throwing; whereas girls are superior in fine motor skills and in balancing. The question asked repeatedly and persistently by motor development specialists is: "What is the basis for these measurable differences?" Some of the answers have already been discussed—namely, that our expectations have been different for the two sexes, even at this young age. With further research, other factors have emerged, such as the fact that the muscle structure of females is different from that of males.

Self-Confidence

In what ways is self-confidence different from competence? At 2½ some children will be fairly competent movers by virtue of their neurological development, size, and/or strength. They may be, or may appear to be, innately more competent than others, yet they may lack the self-confidence to move or to act competently under varying circumstances. Competence, then, may be seen to represent having the ability, whereas self-confidence is being able to put it to use.

How do experiences in the gymnasium contribute to a feeling of self-confidence? An important factor resides in the setup of the equipment. There is equipment with enough variety and degree of difficulty (or ease) so the children can anticipate success. They can choose to go on those pieces of equipment where they know they will be successful. This not only motivates them to move, it also serves to reinforce a feeling of self-confidence. There is intrinsic reinforcement for overt acts. Because they are free to set their own challenges, they have continuous and realistic opportunities to assess themselves. This helps to reinforce the concept of their own ability, and this practice may be as crucial to success as their overt ability per se.

Bruner (1976) states quite perceptively that, "The acts themselves have a self-rewarding character. They are varied systematically, almost as if a play to test the limits of a new skill" (p. 44).

Kinesthetic Awareness

How does the development of this body sense, which is called *kinesthesis*, contribute to psychological development? One answer seems rather obvious: Individuals function as a gestalt, as an integrated whole. Sensations arising from muscles, tendons, and joints (proprioceptors) are integrated with visual and tactile information to give the performer a more complete picture of his or her movement. The choice of the word picture is deliberate. There is strong support for the contention that the development of the motor schema depends largely on the development of vision, on the child's ability to formulate a picture of the environment. And the child whose

Kinesthetic awareness. Turning gives vestibular input of a different kind. Both speed of motion and body position in space are registered by the vestibular and proprioceptive mechanism.

perceptual processes produce a good visual–motor match—that is, seeing the goal and constructing or drawing upon a motor plan to reach that goal—is the child who, like the small boy in our illustration, can run freely without fear of falling or of getting hurt. He can spot the springboard and make a beeline for it. The most important body sense, kinesthesis, contributes to his psychological security.

The information derived from movement, knowledge of performance, is very important in learning to interpret and integrate sensory information. In order to achieve a stable space world, young children need to develop a sense of equilibrium. Although vision contributes to some aspects of equilibrium, most information is derived from the proprioceptors. Once equilibrium is stabilized, other aspects of space, the horizontal and vertical dimensions, can be developed and will make their contributions to the development of laterality and bilateral coordination.

Practice in ducking under apparatus, jumping over it, or getting on and off helps develop a sense of spatial awareness. Such movement lets children find out firsthand whether the pictures they formulate are compatible with their motor plans. If not, then the children formulate other plans, which will work. Their memories become repositories of motor

The versatility of this homemade climbing frame provides practice in being upside-down; in hanging, climbing, and swinging.

plans that can be called into action upon demand. In other words, the children are developing alternative plans of action or composing motor programs that may be generalized to new tasks. We speak of this motor behavior under the rubric of experience.

Yet another contribution that must not be overlooked is the sensuous pleasure derived from moving because it feels good. Being still is anathema to young children. Moving feels wonderful.

Self-Knowledge

Yamamoto (1972) says that the self, as a construct, is more inclusive than the self-concept because it is both the *knower* and the *known*, subject and object. Self-knowledge pertains to both how and what children find out about themselves. So back to the small boy in Chapter 1. He entered the gymnasium, saw the springboard, ran toward it, jumped, performed a forward roll, came up running, and repeated his movement sequence.

Knowledge about the body as subject involves ways in which the body can make movements happen. He ran to the springboard. And he jumped off. These were conscious decisions. He could just as well have seen a ball and thrown it against the wall. Then he might have said to himself: "I can throw the ball. I can control objects in the environment, and I can control my body as well."

He might also have said: "I can make decisions [cognitive] that affect my movements: Climb to the top of the trestle tree." Or "I can run for the sheer joy [affective] of running." "I can control my movement because I am the 'knower' of movements." "I know that I am a feeling, thinking, moving person, and I can make decisions that will result in learning in each of these aspects of my development." "Let me do it." Or, as the young boy on the ski slope said, "Let me do it my way."

But more than this, he might have said: "I am beginning to learn what my body [object] can do. I know I have the strength to let me run fast, to climb high, to jump far. I am beginning to do other, more difficult things. I [subject] have learned these things about myself [object]. I dare to make decisions, to take risks."

Self-knowledge is the vessel that holds the body image, the feelings of competence and confidence. It encompasses what is understood about self-image, decision making, stress, fear of failure, and body awareness. And hopefully, with self-knowledge comes the ability to cope with environmental and personal factors that determine the quality and success of living.

References

KATHERINE READ BAKER, *Let's Play Outdoors* (Washington, D.C.: National Association for the Education of Young Children, 1966).

JEROME S. BRUNER, "Nature and Uses of Immaturity." In J. S. Bruner, A. Jolly, and K. Sylva (Eds.), *Play: Its Role in Development and Evolution* (New York: Basic Books, 1976).

PHILIP PHENIX, *Perceptions of an Ethicist About the Affective* (Washington, D.C.: Association for Supervision and Curriculum Development, 1977).

MIA PRINGLE, *The Needs of Children* (London: Hutchinson of London, 1974).

JEANNE SNODGRASS, "Self-Concept: A Look at its Development and Some Implications for Physical Education Teaching" (Washington, D.C.: *Journal of Physical Education and Recreation*, American Alliance for Health, Physical Education and Recreation, November-December 1977).

Barbara Sprung, *Opening the Options for Children: A Non-Sexist Approach to Early Childhood Education* (Journal of the National Association for the Education of Young Children, November 1975).

Kathy Sylva, Jerome Bruner, and Paul Genova, "The Role of Play in the Problem Solving of Children 3–5 Years Old." In J. S. Bruner and others (Eds.), *Play* (New York: Basic Books, 1976).

R. W. White, "Motivation Reconsidered: The Concept of Competence" (*Psychological Review*, vol. 66, no. 5, 1959).

Kaoru Yamamoto (Ed.), *The Child and His Image, Concept in the Early Years* (Boston: Houghton Mifflin, 1972).

6

Contributions of Active Play to Total Development

What appears to be at stake in play
is the opportunity for assembling
*behavior sequences for skilled action.**

The topic of play as a biological, cultural, or educational phenomenon has challenged many minds during the last two centuries, but to date no synthesized definition has emerged. One might compare play to a diamond of unknown intrinsic value, with psychologists, anthropologists, and sociologists studying different facets, or the same ones with divergent

*From J.S. Bruner, A. Jolly, and K. Sylva, *Play: Its Role in Development and Evolution* (New York: Basic Books, 1976), p. 15. Introduction and Notes © Jerome Bruner, Allison Jolly, and Kathy Sylva, 1976. Reprinted by permission of Basic Books and Penguin Books, Ltd.

What is play?

views, to divine its worth—each discovering describable phenomena without arriving at a cogent definition. Older theories contended that play was an innate capacity, a result of surplus energy, "pleasure-seeking impulse" (Freud), "recapitulatory in nature" (Hall), essentially the expression of a childish nature, "spontaneous" (Froebel, Gesell), a transactional process, "imitative and symbolic" (Piaget). Groos (in Reilly, 1974)* states: "Play was the early manifestation of those instinctive functions which mature during and toward the end of childhood" (p. 63). Froebel (in Castle, 1970) interjects another dimension when he states: "Play is the highest expression of human development in childhood, for it alone is the free expression of what is in a child's soul" (p. 132). And Jersild (1960) adds the concept of self-discovery to his definition: "Play is the way children may move from the known into the untried and unknown" (p. 424). Each of these definitions has some merit for an understanding of the variety of attempts that have been made to define what play is.

*Excerpts from "Defining a Cobweb" by Mary Reilly are reprinted from *Play as Exploratory Learning*, Mary Reilly, ed. Copyright © 1974; by permission of the publisher, Sage Publications, Inc. (Beverly Hills/London).

What, Then, Is Play?

Historically there has been concern for what play is, the kinds of play children engage in, why people—especially children—play, and what the outcome of play may be. The ambiguity of concepts that have emerged provides a parameter of development that has, on the whole, eluded satisfactory treatment until recently, when the work of Bruner, Jolly, and Sylva (1976) spearheaded an enlightened perspective on it as an adaptive function: "Play has the effect of providing practice not so much of survival-relevant instinctive behavior but, rather, of making possible the playful practice of sub-routines of behavior later to be combined in more useful problem-solving" (p. 15).*

This research on play reported by Sylva et al. (1976) has many implications for this book, and Reilly (1974) probably presents the best synthesis and the most comprehensive compilation of ideas about play. She summarizes the present dilemma when she states: "Only the naive could believe from reviewing the evidence of literature, that play is a behavior having an identifiable nature." She herself, as an occupational therapist in quest of an understanding of its significance, iterates several phrases: "Play is a 'connectivity' phenomenon," "a persistent strategy used by man to apprehend the unknown," "to process meaning." Shannon's statement that has the most relevance for understanding young children in the gymnasium is: "Man begins his adventurous response into the unknown by searching for the rules of sensory-motor mastery in the play of his childhood" (p. 297-333).** White (1966), too, has made a meaningful contribution to our understanding: "Play is what the neuromuscular system wants to do when otherwise unoccupied or gently stimulated by the environment".

Development of Play

Reilly establishes three hierarchical stages in the development of play: exploratory, competency, and achievement. The *exploratory* stage occurs during early childhood when there is a confrontation with a new event or object. This evokes the child's capacity to be curious and puzzled. Literature is replete with examples of the behavior of the "terrible two's" who are into everything, and one has only to visit a nursery school to be provided with myriad examples. *Competency* represents the stage of practice with persistence as a driving characteristic. This is consistent with

*From J.S. Bruner, A. Jolly, and K. Sylva, *Play: Its Role in Development and Evolution* (New York: Basic Books, 1976). Intro. and Notes © Jerome Bruner, Allison Jolly, and Kathy Sylva, 1976. Reprinted by permission of Basic Books and Penguin Books, Ltd.

**From *Play as Exploratory Learning*, Mary Reilly, ed. Copyright © 1974; by permission of the publisher, Sage Publications, Inc. (Beverly Hills/London).

White's (1966) notion of a competency drive to deal with the environment, to influence it actively, and to be influenced by it through the feedback mechanism, of which more is said later. This stage is very representative of the children under consideration in this book, for they attack the apparatus in the gymnasium with all the vigor and fearlessness of clowns at a circus as they run, race, and roll for the better part of the period.

Reilly's (1974) third stage, *achievement*, as she describes it, is not applicable because it is linked to a standard of excellence and levels of aspiration that are outside the level of psychomotor development under consideration. With a less arbitrary definition, this stage could also apply. Reilly links achievement to expectancies within the framework of winning and losing—the expectancies children have for themselves as well as those others may hold for them. The older children, particularly the 5-year-olds, are moving in this direction, but since our gymnasium does not present a competitive situation, being better or winning carries little or no significance.* It is evident, at least to this author, that children do have rather well defined expectations for themselves and ones that demand a good deal of courage.

> Billy and June, age 3½, jump off a platform onto a mat five or six times. Then Billy begins to follow his jump with a forward roll each time he lands. June, in imitation, begins to try this movement. She is unable to accomplish the roll but happily and diligently keeps on with the attempt.

June, in this instance, seems to have freedom from the fear of failure; this is different from freedom from failure. This kind of freedom seems to help provide a firm foundation for trying whatever one child sees another one complete. This example lends credence to Shipley and Carpenter's (1962) notion of play as "doing, adventuring, reinforcing, interacting, clarifying, problem solving. In the course of play, thinking is objectified, experiences are intellectualized, and thoughts and emotions are ordered" (p. 19).

In her development of the heuristics of play, Reilly (1974) has some very meaningful concepts for consideration:*

1. Play includes many culturally well-worked activities that a child does because he [or she] is a child. (Liking to swing is an apt example.)
2. Play is an external expression of the developmental product. (Billy's being able to perform a forward roll.)
3. Play relates tasks to capacity and the interactive process to skill. (June could not perform the roll.)

*Excerpts from "Defining a Cobweb" by Mary Reilly are reprinted from *Play as Exploratory Learning,* Mary Reilly, ed. Copyright © 1974; by permission of the publisher, Sage Publications, Inc. (Beverly Hills/London).

4. Play behavior is a mastery process. (Billy was mastering both the jump and the roll.)
5. The major characteristic of the process is fun. ("Fun is something you can do that you like to do"—Evone, age 3.)
6. A major mechanism of playful behavior is imitation. (June following Billy of her own free will) (pp. 152-53).

Play and Development

There seems to be some consensus among other authors, though not without moot points, that play is developmental in character, contributing to physical development and bodily health, emotional stability, intellectual growth, and social cooperation. Piaget (1952) distinguishes between doing something in order to understand what is happening or in order to achieve a new skill, and repeatedly doing it "for fun" (p. 167). Play most certainly may be said to be an exercise in harmonizing or integrating new experiences with past knowledge of achievement. Within the writer's experience, one of the most outstanding features of play is the vitality demonstrated by the players.

Sylva's (1976) characteristics of play are most meaningful at this juncture:

1. The essence of play is in the dominance of means over ends.
2. . . . its lessening the risk of failure.
3. . . . its temporary moratorium on frustration.
4. . . . its invitation to the possibilities inherent in things and events.
5. . . . its voluntary nature. (p. 244)

Play follows a rather normal pattern of development that is largely dependent upon the child's ability to control his or her body and get about. In Erikson's (1971) words: "Child's play begins with the autocosmic . . . centering on his own body. The next step is the microsphere . . . small world of manageable toys. And then the macrosphere which equals the world shared with others (p. 267). Objects, including the body, that are near the infant become the playthings. The body is both object and subject—the plaything and the player simultaneously—and play activity during this stage helps the infant define the "me" and the "not me."

How well I remember the day my namesake made this discovery. It was at the dinner table, and she sat pointing first to me, saying:

"Maida," and then to herself, repeating: "Maida." At first there was a look of puzzlement on her face, and then she began to smile as recognition dawned.

Playing, at this age, is the child's introduction to the reality of the environment. Concepts of hardness and softness, shape and size, all the physical properties of objects that lend themselves to knowledge through manual or visual manipulation, become part of the child's experience. Color, weights, and textures are explored, initially by mouth. Because the mouth is the most sensitive part of the infant's body, it is only natural that it is the best single source of information until the child begins to put together information gathered from eyes and hands. There is a hierarchical organization of the senses, with the sense of touch or movement receptors being the first to supply useful information; later, there is a shift to the predominant use of input from the distance receptors, mainly the eyes for the control of motor behavior.

Significance of Play and Early Play Experiences

In spite of the ambiguity of terms, the significant contributions that play makes to children's development have become increasingly clear during the past decade, as concern about the importance of cognitive learning and the tendency to push children into readiness for academic learning has forced nursery-school teachers and preschool specialists to take a second look at children's needs, and to make more realistic expectations for them. The preschool experience, whether in the nursery school or in the gymnasium, is a valuable and time-consuming involvement that enhances the capacities of the children for fuller living now, but also helps to build a solid foundation for the enrichment and enlargement of later experiences. It is both an end in itself and a means to an end, for the experiences and feelings that are laid down in these early years basically influence subsequent growth and development. White's (1975) research permits him to make a rather forceful statement: "To begin to look at a child's educational development when he is two years of age is already much too late, particularly in the area of social skills and attitudes" (p. 4). Other writers have stressed the importance of laying a good foundation upon which the skills of later years can be built.

The distinction between the personal world and the world around us is the first major contribution of play. And knowledge of the external world is second. The child cannot be taught about the physical properties of objects, because until they become internalized, form images and percepts

Concept of sharing. "Do we have to take turns when the other fellow's lap is so good to sit on?"

in the mind, they have no meaning. And as the player learns about these properties, he or she is also learning about the self, as has been mentioned. Not only is the child distinct from other people and things but he or she is also capable of exploring, manipulating, and discovering independently. This is very sophisticated learning, and much of it happens during the first year.

Millar (1968) has some very descriptive terms for this period under consideration:

> Sensori-motor play as a response to the external world may be sub-divided into exploring, manipulating and practice play. In fact, there are probably at least three different phases involved in "practice" play: . . . exploring play as a reaction to novel stimulus patterns, manipulating play which itself produces whatever changes there may be; and repetition or repetition with variation. The latter may serve to integrate the experience with the rest of the organism's know -how (pp. 108, 134).

As mobility increases, the player establishes a wider and wider range of play activity, and a shift takes place that includes actively playing with people. The ambulatory player now learns to explore, to discover, and especially to manipulate other people—parents at first and then peers. This is the third significant contribution to the child's development.

> Timmy, 2½ years old, plays contentedly by the side of the pool. Gradually he becomes bold enough to venture down the first step. This gains applause from the attending adults, so he ventures down the second step. The water now comes midway up his belly. With the third step, the closest parent jumps to be sure he does not take one more, which would lead to water over his head. Descending the stairs now becomes a game that Timmy plays with great delight.

Play will take several forms before it becomes truly cooperative, and these lead ultimately through the gamut of social interaction.

The period of the posttoddler is the peak period of exploration. Many 2½-year-olds are still more comfortable playing alone or with an adult than they are with peers. By 5 years of age, however, most children have reached the cooperative stage—if not all the time, at least for a significant portion, and if not in all activities, then for those identified as most important to getting along in preschool. In the gymnasium, the older children have become quite sociable and are really quite quick to help each other, which is a highly developed perception of another's needs. An older tot will hold the rope for a younger one or give a hand to the cautious descent of someone near. There is much for us to learn about the way they help each other.

A fourth significant contribution is in the realm of ideas. Infants play with sounds as they learn to vocalize and with words as they learn to talk. When they are capable of expressing concepts and ideas, they follow the same sequence of exploration, manipulation, and discovery as with things and people. We see this particularly in the gymnasium, where they will invent any number of ways to use a single piece of apparatus. They have no preconceived notion of how it should be used; and they fear no censor, as older children may, so they invent to their heart's content. Here again they are involved in the dual nature of play: They are simultaneously object and subject. They manipulate their bodies over a piece of apparatus, thus discovering not only what can be performed on a particular piece but also what their bodies can perform on that particular piece. And here they learn about strength, agility, coordination, flexibility, and balance. Perhaps the greatest contribution of playing in the gymnasium is in the realm of self-knowledge, as discussed before.

When playing, the child is making his or her own experiences; a small child just doesn't have the vocabulary to learn from others. The process of playing is as important as the product, as with problem solving, for there may be no castle of blocks or sand, no doughy gingerbread man or firechief going to a fire. The scooter does readily convert into a fire truck and the pole into a fireman's pole; but on the whole, children are too absorbed with the apparatus itself to feel the need to convert it into something imaginary. The intangible product is a reservoir of experiences—in this case, neuromuscular ones—very personal ones that may never be replicated but that represent what the child has tried and succeeded at or tried and found wanting. The child who persistently tries to wiggle through a tunnel may have to try and try again until the motor plan coincides with her or his visual image of the passageway.

> Lise, age 3½, kept putting all the balls back into the box as soon as one was tossed out. Scarcely another child had a chance to play with these brightly colored balls, for their being spread around the gym seemed to offend Lise's sense of tidiness.

Prehensile coordination is gained through this kind of manipulative behavior, and nursery schools are replete with potential experiences of this kind. Play in the gymnasium also fosters, encourages, and develops manipulative performance. The object manipulated may be the child's own body, but what could be more functional to an understanding of oneself and one's world?

Taking things apart helps children see relationships so that they can eventually put things together again. Undressing, for example, is easy because the outer layer comes off first. But what goes on first? Which side is up or right side out? A very easy way to help the child put on a coat is by laying it on the floor with the neck toward the child and face upward. The child then puts hands in the sleeves, taking it over the head, and it is in its proper place for buttoning or zipping. Trials with the right and left shoe, mitten, or coat sleeve lead to concepts of rightness and leftness and to the final establishment of eye, hand, and foot dominance. What at first is very much a puzzlement to young children becomes slowly untangled with sufficient adventure, practice, curiosity, and imagination. So, too, in the gymnasium. Concepts of up and down, in and out, right and left may be explored until they form a meaningful basis for understanding how the body works and what it is capable of doing under a variety of conditions demanding gross and sometimes fine movements.

Children also learn the consequences of their play in many instances, and this is different from the products of play. Running through a puddle is fun, and you may or may not get wet. Playing with mud may be even more fun, but you may get spanked if you get dirty. So being dirty and being spanked are different consequences. If the child is also learning to be responsible for his or her behavior, then play presents a fallow ground for sowing the seeds of self-directed discipline.

Children appear to have no fear, and most of the time they really don't, because they do not know the consequences.

A 3-year-old who could swim put on a diver's mask when he saw his father scuba diving and jumped into the water without realizing that he had to learn to breathe with the mask on. Once the snorkel was put in his mouth and he learned to use it, he was "safe" in the water. He had no fear because he did not know the difference between swimming on the surface and underwater.

Gradually, with enough experience and/or guidance, some of the outcomes of play become manifest to the player; for example, when you play with dough, you may be making cookies.

Playing with ideas—that is, thinking—is without doubt, in our society at least, the most productive and best rewarded kind of playing. At this age, children are beginning to anticipate: If I climb that ladder, I can drop between the rungs to the floor or hang by my knees. The older ones can even tell you how they can change something like rolling round like a ball or straight like a log; whereas the younger ones can only show you, because they do not yet have a descriptive vocabulary. The 5-year-olds begin to

Weightlessness is experienced at the height of Sonia and Amy's jump. Friends learn from each other.

know that to spin fast, one needs to keep the body close to its axis and that to slow down, one spreads the extremities out. The youngest will spin until they fall down from lack of equilibrium, but the oldest can decelerate the spin and remain on balance. This is ideational game playing. These changes in action-knowledge and action-anticipation are important to almost any avenue of life, and the gymnasium is a place where example after motor example is evident. These are the ones that young children integrate first into their perceptual schema. How children choose to play within this setting is conditioned by the concerted components of their psychomotor, cognitive, and emotional development.

Give your pupils liberty, then, as in a garden planted with situations carefully devised to give them many freedoms to jump, to run, to make noise, to observe and to use freely all the opportunities suggested in the challenging objects around them.

E. B. CASTLE (1970)*

References

JEROME BRUNER in Jerome S. Bruner, Alison Jolly, and Kathy Sylva, *Play: Its Role in Development and Evolution* (New York: Basic Books, 1976).

E. B. CASTLE, *The Teacher* (New York: Oxford University Press, 1970).

ERIK ERIKSON in R. E. Heron and Brian Sutton-Smith, *Child's Play* (New York: John Wiley and Sons, Inc., 1971).

A. JERSILD, *Child Psychology* (6th ed.) (Englewood Cliffs, NJ: Prentice-Hall, 1966).

SUSANNA MILLAR, *The Psychology of Play* (New York: Penguin Books, 1968).

JEAN PIAGET, *Play & Imitations in Childhood* (London: Heinemann, 1951).

FERN SHIPLEY and ETHELOUISE CARPENTER, *Freedom to Move* (Washington, D.C.: National Education Association, Department of Elementary–Kindergarten–Nursery Education, 1962).

KATHY SYLVA, JEROME BRUNER, and PAUL GENOVA, "The Role of Play in the Problem Solving of Children 3–5 Years Old." In Bruner and others (Eds.), *Play* (New York: Basic Books, 1976).

BURTON WHITE, *The First Three Years of Life* (Englewood Cliffs, NJ: Prentice-Hall, Inc., 1975).

ROBERT W. WHITE, "Motivation Reconsidered: The Concept of Competence" (*Psychological Review*, vol. 66, no. 5, 1959).

*From E.B. Castle, *The Teacher* (New York: Oxford University Press, 1970).

The teacher as trustee
of the child's capacity for self-direction.

SIGNIFICANT OTHERS:

The Teachers,
Parents, Peers,
Playground Directors,
Teacher's Aides

7

The Role
of Significant
Others

*If generalized self-esteem is to be enhanced and maintained,
children need teachers who are accepting,
who make them feel secure, who have realistic clear
behavioral expectations, and who encourage
independence and responsibility.*

The central concern of this chapter is with the roles that people—including teachers, parents, aides, playground directors and older children—play in a gymnasium, backyard, or playground with very young children. The sensitivity, imagination, and teaching skills that are discussed are those Torrance and Myers (1974) label higher-order ones, which are not easily developed. The traditional roles of instruction, socialization, and evalua-

*From Shirley Samuels, *Enhancing Self-Concept in Early Childhood* (New York: Human Sciences Press, 1977), p. 184.

tion, which teachers play or play at, are important both for discussion and elaboration. However, the more subtle behaviors and functions that have been implicit expectations are made explicit in this chapter.

One of the major objectives is to evoke creative behavior, a form of behavior that, according to Torrance and Myers (1974), has to be learned. Since these are the years during which children need plenty of practice in gross motor activities and little, if any, formal instruction, other facets of the teaching—learning situation are examined for contributions to this learning process.

The child, as Rousseau, Pastalozzi, and Froebel (in Castle, 1970) pointed out so emphatically, is the center of attention. Knowledge of child development; motor development; how the child thinks, behaves, moves, and, perhaps more important, how he or she feels while moving are of paramount significance. Also inherent in this educational process is knowledge of interpersonal relations and a sense of the value of purposeful activity that often reaches strenuosity.

When they feel free, they can give unbridled play to their innate curiosity and problem-solving ability. The teacher, sitting watchfully on the periphery, aims to foster the desires for self-direction and to capitalize on intrinsically motivated activity that will produce learning. The teacher cherishes the fact that children can be and often are, by themselves, self-initiated and self-initiating learners.

And it behooves us to stop and think about the role of other children, particularly those who are a year or two older, with larger and more highly developed repertoires of motor skills. Among a group of young children, the most significant question is how to create this atmosphere for learning. Other questions are: "Who are the models for learning?" "What teaching skills are most important?" "How is this very special teacher trained?" Since a rather large part of children's time is spent relating to their peers, let us begin this examination of the learning environment by focusing on these most important peers.

Older Children as Models

> Children learn more from other children than they do
> from teachers, who should be catalysts for discovery.
>
> HAROLD LYON (1971)*

One has only to be on a ski slope watching the younger child follow a sibling, or to observe children playing together in nearly any situation to

*From Harold C. Lyon, Learning to Feel and Feeling to Learn (Columbus, OH: Charles E. Merrill Publishing Co., 1971).

realize the "teaching" capacity of older children. Their language is often more relevant, their explanations more terse, and their expectations more realistic than those of some adults. The younger child demonstrates a blotterlike capacity for being taught, and the older child seems to need to demonstrate his or her own superior competence; so focus for a moment on peers as model teachers and as models in their own way.

Adam was 3 and his brother 2. It was such fun watching Adam try to explain and demonstrate how to get a playground ball over a volleyball net "because it happened to be there." One on a side, the "teacher" held the ball behind his head and heaved with all his might to an ineffectual height, hitting the net in the middle and rebounding to the tosser. "You stand this way," said Adam with his feet together. "You hold the ball behind your head like this," expostulated the 3-year-old sage, trying again with increased success at achieving height. The goal seemed obvious to the 2-year-old. Adam changed his distance from the net by moving nearer and thus was able to toss even higher. Meanwhile his brother waited patiently for his turn, which finally came when the ball inadvertently went under the net.

Neither child in the foregoing illustration accomplished the goal of getting the ball over the net, but we must pause and look for the moment at concomitant learnings. Adam certainly learned something about space when he moved closer to the net. He also learned about force as he made the ball go increasingly higher. He was modeling, satisfying a need to demonstrate competence while his brother was attending, developing listening and seeing skills. Both were engaged in learning how to learn. Children are intuitively sensitive to their own needs, so they determine what the optimum time spent in "instruction" or practice is to be. We adults may feel that there is insufficient detail in the presentation. For example, Adam said nothing about placing the hands behind the ball. Or we may feel that the information is incorrect: Adam's feet were together; but we must remember that young children often focus on the goal rather than on the process of achieving it and therefore have a global image of what has to be done. As a colleague of the author's says: "They need to get the *picture* [image or goal], get the *message* [motor plan], and *get to work* [practice]." What they really need at this age is time for practice, time to grow, and time to enjoy what they are doing. Details will come later, when they become more meaningful and more necessary.

A small boy was riding the ski lift behind me when I heard him say to his companion, who was obviously a ski instructor: "But I don't want a lesson." This statement was loaded with as much feeling as the

4-year-old could give it. The instructor replied quite matter-of-factly: "But your father wants you to learn to ski." To which the child responded with increased feeling: "I want to do it my way." His goal was to get down the slope. His father's goal was for him to ski "correctly."

What is "correct" for age 4? Similarly, a 3-year-old girl was followed by the author as she zigzagged down the slope in her slow, snowplow, serpentine course. She was observed from a distance by an extremely knowledgeable and tolerant mother. With her low center of gravity, a characteristic of all small children, her danger of being hurt if she fell was minimal; and her flyweight made her descent more like that of a huge, slow moth, caressing the top of each mogul it passed. With more weight, and hence more speed, this little girl will need to learn the finer points of skiing, and then she will be ready for more formal teaching.

Motor patterns change with age, as limbs grow longer and body proportions change. The developmental form of running of the 3-year-old, for example, is different from that of the preadolescent, and time—not teaching—is necessary for some changes to take place. Because young children's legs are relatively short, their rhythmic patterns of walking and running are very rapid and percussive. The 4- or 5-year-old, acting as a visual model, is performing at nearly eye level as opposed to the adult, who is "way up there." The auditory pattern of the model may also be something that younger children can imitate either consciously or unconsciously. And the fun of the game element, of playing "teacher and pupil" with other children, cannot be minimized. Can't you remember playing school? Perhaps of equal importance is the fact that the model learns as he or she explains or demonstrates. Very young children will run faster when being chased and will throw farther and higher when being chased and when levers are longer and muscles stronger; time and the practice of emerging skills are what they really need. Montessori (1966) called this a "period of sensitivity of development," and she stressed two things—the child's innate ability to push through with a task until deciding that it had come to its conclusion, and a conviction that these periods could be made to happen. White (1975), addressing the acquisition of motor skills, says that young children will practice until they get them right.

How well I remember 3-year-old Paul, who spent the entire gym period climbing the three steps of a platform and jumping off without so much as a rest period. One of his nursery-school teachers asked me, if he shouldn't be stopped or changed to another activity. To which I replied: "Why? Let's see what he does next time." Sure enough, he

Peer assistance: Amy helping Sonia. Over, under, around, and through—you help me, and I'll help you.

tried a variety of activities. His period of sensitivity to jumping had diminished.

And Amy comes to mind as another example of this very personal period of sensitivity.

At 3, she is scarcely as tall as the balance beam she chooses to climb on and walk across. Upon jumping off, she performs first one, then a dozen forward rolls across the mat—more as though she had tumbled from her mother's womb than been delivered in a conventional way. She does, in fact, have two older brothers whom she loves to imitate, so this is an excellent example of modeling.

Since time with the peer group comprises such a large percent of playing time, we must consider very seriously the contributions that peers make to learning. It is more than taking advantage of a situational factor. It involves consciously and conscientiously planning that learning does come about with peers as models.

References

E. B. CASTLE, *The Teacher* (New York: Oxford University Press, 1970).

Montessori in Perspective (Washington, D.C.: Publications Committee of the National Association for the Education of Young Children, 1966).

E. PAUL TORRANCE and R. E. MYERS, *Creative Learning & Teaching* (New York: Dodd, Mead & Co., 1974).

BURTON L. WHITE, *The First Three Years of Life* (Englewood Cliffs, N.J.: Prentice-Hall, Inc., 1975).

ROBERT W. WHITE, *"Motivation Reconsidered: The Concept of Competence"* (*Psychological Review*, vol. 66, no. 5, 1959).

8

The Role
of Adults

*Authority wisely exercised reinforces
the pupil's capacity to contribute to his own growth.* *

Skilled Intervention

What constitutes "authority" within the context of the gymnasium or
playground setting where the performers are 2½- to 5-year-old children?
One of the major concerns teachers and parents must have is for the safety
of the children, and one element of safety is control. The authority figure

*Attributed to Johann Pestalozzi in E.B. Castle, *The Teacher* (New York: Oxford University
Press, 1970).

has to be in control. And one facet of control is discipline. Never has it been a more crucial problem; never have all teachers and parents needed to be more understanding of its necessity, its form, and its implications.

The transition from a focus on external control to one on internal or self-control is one of the most significant pedagogical changes in teaching young children today. Movement education—with its focus on self-learning—poses problems of self-discipline for the pupil, for the new teacher, and for the teacher/parent who is working with very young children for the first time. The pupil must learn and be charged with the responsibility to determine what constitutes acceptable behavior for a learning environment. The teacher/parent must help with these determinations but must discipline her- or himself to let children make their own mistakes unless there is a safety factor involved.

It is important for all teachers, parents, aides, and playground directors to understand that children's behavior is determined by the notions they hold about themselves—who they are, how well they like themselves, where they are going. This is no less true for teachers/parents. And how are these notions established? By experimenting and exploring, probing and protecting, trying and testing, discovering and discarding.

How can we apply the apparent paradox of tough and tender to the concept of discipline? It may first be applied to the notion of how one knows who one is. Children often find out about themselves by trying you, the teacher/parent—by challenging, rebuking, and testing you—especially if you are new. Sometimes all they want to hear is, "Stop it. Now!" To which they may reply: "OK" and grin. Many of them need to have something concrete to hit at—a rule to challenge, a game to play, a person to confront. They are like a small boy I knew who would punch the wall with his fist, finding out simultaneously the toughness of the wall and his own strength. Toughness testing toughness.

On the tender side, children need to know that you understand them, that you accept them, that you like them. They will know this when you listen to what they really say in all their childish candor. At the same time they need to know the distinction between your accepting them and accepting their behavior. When they know you understand and like them, you can be tough with their behavior. They really want you to expect them to behave well, just as they really want to behave well.

When you let children know that you like them, and most of them know instinctively that you do, you help them like themselves. When they like themselves, they in turn can be tough with their own behavior. At the same time, they learn to accept themselves. The environment that fosters this kind of critical self-analysis with acceptance, tough yet tender, also nurtures self-discipline and promotes self-determined growth in the ability to take responsibility.

Today's world is a tough one for children, besetting them with pressures, bombarding them with decisions. The teacher who helps children to be successful with small responsibilities fosters feelings of status that help them know where they are and where they are going. By designing the toughness of tasks so that success is inevitable, the "can concept" is enhanced.

Most children can do far more than we think, and many of them know it. Moreover, most of them like things tough. Nothing seems to pull them up to a high level of performance faster than the statement: "This is very difficult." They call, "That's easy," before they start to try. This is another way of saying that children like to be stretched, to be challenged. Few discipline problems arise when all are working their hardest to solve a problem. If the problem is one of their own making, you can be sure they know where they want to go.

Teacher as Interpreter and Monitor

Speech is not a skill one acquires on one's own;
it is a complex mysterious ability dependent on contact
and interaction with an attentive adult
RUTH INGLIS (1973)*

Today we are beginning to understand the importance of the early acquisition of language and motor skills, and that there is a relationship between them. Inglis (1973), writing about the urgent need for language learning in the earliest years, states: "Today we know that if a child does not hear or imitate the sounds of an attentive adult before he is three years old, he may never acquire the ability to speak" (p. 30).* The same might be said about the acquisition of fundamental motor skills. If there is ample opportunity to develop these when the child is maturationally ready, their acquisition is relatively easy; if delayed, the learning process becomes more difficult. And this relationship between motor skill development and language acquisition has only begun to be studied. Kephart and Godfrey (1969) say that when learning is difficult, "more intensive and extensive learning experiences are required for mastery of the skills involved. Unless such additional learning experience is provided, the developmental processes involved in this stage are apt to be inadequately established (p. 182).

The physical activity of young children, particularly in the gymnasium, is replete with action words, as mentioned before: *run, jump, slide,*

*Excerpted from the book *A Time to Learn* by Ruth Inglis. Copyright © 1973 by Ruth Inglis. Reprinted by permission of The Dial Press.

spin, and *twist.* Their use, either by other children or especially by an adult, reinforces language skills. Though they may be too young to understand syntax or word forms per se, with thought on the teacher's part, ordinal and cardinal numbers, adverbs, and adjectives can easily be a worthwhile part of the gymnasium experience and a more meaningful contribution to subsequent storytelling or discussion. With a little more thought, synonyms and antonyms can be interjected as children move in order to describe how they move or how they might move differently. Luria's (1961) point that "adequate active speech, and its sequel, internal speech, can modify behavior" (p. 199), is one to be kept in mind if the teacher wishes to enhance the acquisition of langauge *and* skills of movement.

> Jason began coming to the gym at 27 months of age. The first time he came, he climbed every ladder. Up, down, up, down. In subsequent visits, he climbed, swung on ropes, jumped, slid down slides, hung, rolled, and was much more diverse in his activity. He was just 3 when the gymnastic tryouts for the Olympic Games were televised. Thinking that he might like to see the apparatus activity, his father suggested that he watch. After a glance, his remark was: "I don't need to look; we learned all that in gym."

The equipment in the gymnasium—ropes, ladder, bench, box—all acquire meaning as well. The teacher's role is to name, to model, to repeat, to reinforce, and to monitor language and motor skills because of their significance to total development. It is also necessary for the teacher to *listen.* Teachers must develop what Moustakas (1972) terms "sensitive listening." They must not merely listen to words but also listen intently both to the way words are spoken and, as is often the case, to what words are left out—not spoken but implied.

> Tracy was a beautiful, redheaded, freckled-nosed 4-year-old who, upon seeing me, asked if I was the gym teacher. "Rather old," said she, which really made me smile. Yet later, seeing me in my gym clothes for the first time, she took my hand, saying: "You're not as old as I thought you were." Together we skipped down the hall. Too old to teach her? Too old to teach gym? What was she saying?

Skilled Nonintervention

> *The essence of the teacher's task is to cooperate*
> *with the developing sense, observation and reason*
> *progressively emerging in the pupil.*
> ROUSSEAU

Teacher as Cooperator

Cooperation is, indeed, like a coin with two identifiable sides—heads and tails. Teachers and parents, authority figures, usually expect children to cooperate with them, so what are some of the connotations of the other side of the coin? What particular meaning does the Rousseauian definition have for us? Within the setting of the gymnasium, much of this cooperation takes place in planning for the setup of equipment at the developmental level of the young children. The goals that direct this planning may be different from those of the classroom, but the exercise of planning with care is no different. Colors of balls and other small, manipulable equipment are bright and eye-catching to enhance the children's developing sense of visual discrimination, and to permit them to learn to make choices that have a variety of bases. "I want a blue ball," one youngster cries. "I want the biggest one," says another, as she equates the heaviness of one sixteen-inch playground ball with size in the best Piagetian sense. What is heavy is also large until there has been sufficient opportunity to discover otherwise. These experiences are carefully planned by the astute teacher.

In fact, colors of mats and selected pieces of equipment must take into account children's developing sense of figure-ground as well, so the single mat or piece of apparatus will stand out clearly against the floor and not cause a particular child to stumble and fall. Some children are ground dependent and need practice in distinguishing colors and objects, especially since they are almost always in a hurry. The ability to select and track are prerequisite skills for catching bean bags or balls; the ability to select figures and to follow lines is also necessary for reading. Objects of different shapes must be included, as well as those with varying colors. Three- and 4-year-olds tend to rely on shapes or forms for identification of objects, but by the age of 5, color plays a more dominant role. This seems to be a critical time for increasing motivation for motor performance through the use of color.

And the tactile sense is another one to be planned for. In a very sensitive article about the Fore children of New Guinea, entitled "In Touch and Free," Sorenson (1977) comments on child-rearing practices and the importance of the tactile sense:*

> The transmission of the Fore behavioral patterns to the young began in early infancy during a period of unceasing human physical contact. . . . While very young, infants remained in almost continuous contact with their mother . . . remaining in close, uninterrupted contact with those around them, their basic needs such as rest, nourishment, stimulation and security were satisfied without obsta-

*From E. Richardson Sorenson, "In Touch and Free: Growing Up as a FORE Is to Be In Touch and Free." Copyright 1977 Smithsonian Institution, from *Smithsonian* magazine, May 1977.

cle. They had kinesthetic contact with the activities at hand . . . [which] made it easy for them to learn the appropriate handling of the tools of life. . . . In close harmony with their source of life, the Fore young were able confidently, not furtively, to extend their inquiry. (pp. 106-14)

The tactile sense has been for all young children, and continues to be for some, the dominant sense. True, a major objective of early learning is to help children utilize other senses within the hierarchy, so that they depend less on touch and more and more on the information provided through seeing, hearing, and proprioception. However, until the child feels that the yellow yarn ball is soft and fuzzy, how can he or she see that it is? There is much for us to learn about the contributions of body surfaces to information gathering. Why do children like to slide down a slide on their bellies? Because they do like to stunt, to go headfirst, or because it feels good on that particular part of their anatomy? Both reasons are valid ones. Certainly much of the sensory information garnered from belly-bump and seat sliding is different, but what it contributes to learning we can only speculate.

We do know that the soles of the feet and palms of the hands are two most sensitive areas, next only to the mouth. This is reason enough to have the children barefooted. Thus their small toes can grip a ladder; the sole of the foot can adhere enough to permit the owner to walk up a slide, balance on a beam, or come to a stop more quickly than with slippery shoes or socks. Since the act of stopping, together with changing directions, has to be learned and practiced, whatever factors facilitate this should be considered in planning.

Covering surfaces such as a balance beam or box with carpeting not only changes the "feel" to bare feet; it may, in fact, give the child more security and thus change the activity being performed. Plan for slippery surfaces for sliding and spinning, smooth surfaces for holding and gripping, and uneven surfaces for touching. Plastic balls have quite a different feel from rubber playground ones; they are lighter and respond differently. Of course, they cannot be sat upon or balanced on as the large, popular, sixteen-inch ones can, but they do lend themselves more readily to bouncing and dribbling or even kicking.

All movement tasks make demands on the sensory-motor mechanism of the body. Speaking has its demands on the vocal cords and muscles of the throat; writing exacts coordination of the muscles of the fingers, which interpret what the child is to write. In a developmental sense, the activities of the gymnasium should precede or be a vital part of the nursery-school program, because—as stated before—the large-proximal or gross muscles of upright posture are neurologically capable of action before the fine ones. Therefore it is evident that more emphasis should be placed upon gross motor activities. Many nursery schools do have rather extensive equipment, such as scooters and climbing frames, and do devote a rather large amount of time to out-of-door activity. However, it has been the experience of this author that those persons responsible for the conduct of these programs do not understand the relative importance of gross motor development and its possible facilitation of fine motor development. Because writing, a fine motor skill, is prerequisite to successful school experience, those manipulative activities that may contribute to a more successful experience are well provided for. Those large motor activities that may contribute to a lifetime of skillful movement have either been neglected altogether or relegated to a minor role.

Most of the provisions for large muscle activity demand space. The notion that small children should be confined to small spaces probably had its inception among architects who related size of child with size of space. But children need big, unimpeded space—free space in which to run as fast as the wind and stop just before crashing into the wall. Dodging, fleeing, and catching are part of the game, as mothers of toddlers know only too well when their children first learn to escape. Good health—which this large muscle activity promotes—plenty of space, and a supportive adult are three ingredients that practically ensure that young children will develop most of the fundamental motor skills to a proficient degree. To plan for the space and to be the supportive adult—this, then, constitutes cooperative teaching. The teacher can always feel the pulse of the activity, is always involved as an informed observer. Under the keen eye of a cooperating adult who has provided situations of optimum stimulation, young children appear to grow and bloom most happily.

Teacher as Facilitator

> Observe the phenomena for growth in their infinite variety;
> feed his curiosity;
> watch, refrain, encourage, guide without seeming to.
>
> ROUSSEAU

To facilitate is to make learning easy.

"Can you skip?" I asked 2½-year-old Shelly.
"That's easy," she replied while showing me.
"Where did you learn?" I asked with temerity.
"I always knew!" she said with confidence.

To facilitate is also to make it fun, with some of the same bouyancy and certainly with the same sense of confidence that Shelly had. Few 2½-year-olds can skip; most of them do a step, then a step, hop—more like a gallop.

It was Shelly who, at 2, went straight over the top of a ten-foot ladder with a determination not to be stopped and with no fear of consequences. Running faster, throwing farther, climbing higher are overt signs of physical growth or development in which the physical educator usually revels, partly because they represent changes in behavior that may represent learning. They may also represent maturation—that Siamese twin of growth that makes learning possible—for until the processes of neuromuscular maturation have taken place, learning is either impossible or more difficult.

Most assuredly, the major role of the teacher is *not* presenting "skills" for young children to "learn." In a way the roles are reversed, for it is the children who present skills and the teacher who watches—watches to see the limitless variety of skills or variations on a single skill, watches to help the timid and shy or to beware of the bold and brave.

> David was about to go over the top of the Swedish window ladder. The vigilant eye of the teacher was able to catch his eye just in time to arrest the movement. No one had ever climbed to the top before, so the rule not to go over had to be enacted on the spot.

Ostler and Kranz (1976) write: "A great deal of what children express is transmitted through nonverbal channels such as eye contact, gestures, particular facial expressions, intonations, energy changes, or even a postural stance" (p. 113). David was communicating his sense of boldness from the top of the ladder through a definite nonverbal channel. Nonverbal cues have a very potent influence on adult–child understandings and actions. It is through these understandings and transactions that teaching and learning, especially in the gymnasium where pupil–teacher interaction in a formal sense may be at a minimum, go forward.

How many of us watch and really see? Listen and really hear? Ask and really question? Answer and really respond? These skills of attending, observing, and questioning demand an almost undivided attention, and when is a teacher's attention ever undivided? But the skills can be practiced, and they are ones that need to be honed razor sharp if one is to cope with the rapidity of development and change in young children. Their questions are so immediate, so varied, and so unexpected. "May I climb the rope to see what the ceiling looks like from up there?" How does one prepare for this? Their energy is so ebullient and boundless. How does one monitor this? Their activity, so explosive and unpredictable. How does one guide this?

The skills of attending, observing, questioning, and listening are ones with a very high priority for the children to learn as well, so it is wise for the teacher to model this very special behavior. Because there is always risk involved when children are on large apparatus, it is especially important for both children and teacher to be aware and alert in the gymnasium. Children understand this need when it is explained to them.

"Help me on the rope," one child requests. But the other ten, twelve, or twenty may need help if you do. "Step on my knee, and climb up yourself," says the teacher. "Take me down," says another. "Try putting your foot here, and see if you can't get down by yourself," the teacher replies. There is always a response from the teacher, but it may not be the same one the parent might give on a playground, with a one-to-one relationship. Usually the child who can climb up can also find a way to climb down, and the wise teacher rarely lifts up or takes down. How do you really want to help the child—to become dependent and scared, or independent and secure? Parents at a playground are presented with a different problem, but the teacher can never forget the responsibility and safety of the rest of the children. Besides these replies, what does constitute encouragement or help? A hand extended to the child crossing the balance beam for the first time. The child is free to take or not take the hand, and the teacher's presence constitutes encouragement enough with most children. Or sometimes a hug will do. "You did it! I knew you could." Verbal as well as nonverbal language—like a smile or a pat on the back—can be a wonderful tool for praise, encouragement, and guidance.

What is being said here is that the facilitator is supportive of children's decisions. Overtly by saying, "You choose which rope to hang from," and covertly by watching which rope the child does choose, the facilitator encourages the process of decision making and supports the product, standing by to offer help if the particular decision turns out to be just a little bit over the child's head. It is impossible to rule out "poor," "improper," or "bad" decisions, and there is an important challenge in difficult ones, especially when they turn out to reflect growth in both the process and product of decision making. What is of utmost importance is to enhance the child's ability to choose wisely by deleting impossible or unsafe choices. These are judgments the wise, experienced teacher is competent to make.

Positioning of the teacher's body next to apparatus can denote confidence or apprehension to young children.

> The mother of a 14-month-old child stood behind her while she climbed up the steps of the five-foot ladder and sat down at the top of the slide. Then the mother moved to the bottom of the slide, where the child joyfully slid with great confidence.

Judicious positioning? Most certainly, it facilitated both the performance and the enjoyment. If the teacher, or parent, for that matter, has any apprehension whatsoever about a particular piece of equipment, it should not be used, for this feeling can be contagious; and the only feeling worth communicating in the gymnasium is one of confidence. The apprehensive teacher has no place in the gymnasium in the first place or, in fact, in charge of young children, for this quality or feeling tends to restrict activity rather than facilitate its development. But isn't this a bit unrealistic? Won't children get hurt? Not if the selection of equipment is sound in the first place. When mats are judiciously placed and the original planning has taken into account the safety factors by establishing adults near any particularly high pieces, both children and adults have a realistic sense of security. Teachers as well as children can learn confidence.

> My first experience with a group of very young children in the gymnasium involved setting out apparatus that was, on the whole, close to the floor and safe. The highest piece was only as high as the tallest 4-year-old. And were they bored! The children spent most of the time running around the equipment or sitting in the laps of the teaching aides. The very next time, the apparatus was at least twice as high, and the children responded like clowns at a circus. Now a twenty-foot Swedish window ladder and an eight-foot trestle tree are but two of the heights to which they may climb with my blessing and confidence and with their courage and competence.

If the role of facilitator appears to be a passive one, then some clarification is in order. The teacher must watch with *intent to remember* what ten, twelve, or twenty young children do in order to set up the gymnasium for their changing needs the next time. What changes will both arouse their curiosity and meet their needs? The question is like a double-edged sword: What have the children learned, and what changes can be made to facilitate further learning? In the gym as in the classroom, a child's readiness for subsequent developmental tasks depends in large measure on her or his successful management of the tasks of the preceding stage. White (1975) assumes that normal motor skill acquisition will take place, but Kephart (1969) states that because this assumption is shared by many parents and teachers, intensification of these experiences under the skilled eye of a trained teacher is the best insurance in helping children with tasks that are necessary for smooth movement from stage to stage. Within the context of cognitive development, Bruner (1973) says, "Three is already too late" (p. 133). It is already too late for the acquisition of some of the fundamental motor skills, such as walking.

Changes in behavior can be noted: The 3-year-old who, on the second try, does a forward roll following her jump from the springboard appears to have learned. But what did she learn about balance, body position, rotary motion? Will she be able to repeat the movement sequence next week? Or tomorrow? The major concern is what activity or piece of apparatus will challenge this particular child next. Oh, the master challenge of having, twelve or even twenty different children ages 2½ to 5. One guiding principle must be borne in mind at all times, for it is so easy to exploit children who do precocious things: Don't make a child's future the criterion of your teaching or planning, but what that child needs *now*, for this particular moment of development toward stability.

To be a facilitator, the teacher must be a very keen observer. What are some of the things to look for? Wickstrom (1977) has synthesized the material on the development of motor patterns, and his suggestions at the end of each chapter are a worthwhile place for the teacher to start. These are the details of the fundamental motor patterns of running, jumping, catching, throwing, kicking, and striking. Young children will be attempting all of these with varying degrees of success, so the various developmental forms should be imprinted on the teacher's mind. Sinclair (1973) gives age guidelines for twenty-five selected movement tasks and discusses the following characteristics common to many tasks: opposition and symmetry, dynamic balance, total body assembly, rhythmic two-part locomotion, eye–hand efficiency in manual response to static or moving objects, agility, postural adjustment, and dominance. Her charts are self-explanatory, and teachers should be well acquainted with them in order to observe the characteristics of developing movement patterns.

This author is concerned with some of the finer points of movement, such as the use of hands and toes in gripping the rungs of a ladder or climbing frame. Is the thumb used in opposition to the fingers for a more secure grip, or is the hand too small for such a rung? Do the toes grip the edge of the beam or springboard so the child, upon jumping, will not slip backward? Children think nothing of jumping from the high balance beam, whether or not there is a protective mat. And barefooted landings demand more care, lest the foot be hurt. Children seem to know this instinctively.

Does the small girl close her eyes when trying to catch the ball? Or even when she throws it? Why do so many children appear to have flat feet? Will this tendency disappear as the feet are strengthened by running, jumping, and gripping? Note the beautiful extension of the child on the scooter and of the one who just jumped. Where is this kind of astute observation discussed? Certainly not in the literature on young children, which has been, until recently, completely devoid of discussion of the significance of gross motor development to very young children. Interest in its importance begins with teachers—astute teachers with patience, imagination, and a thorough knowledge of all facets of child development.

Teachers as Transmitters of Values

> *Cultivate each child's understanding of himself and his world*
> *by his own discriminating and self-imposed activity.*
>
> E. B. CASTLE (1970)*

Children begin to learn what patterns of behavior are expected of them even before entering the gymnasium, for they have their own grapevine communication system from year to year that is far more effective than anything adults could tell them. What could you possibly tell a 2½-year-old that would prepare him or her for all the excitement of swinging, sliding, and spinning? They are told only to take off their socks and shoes, for bare feet are mandatory. Therein lies one of the first values to be imparted in the total experience. Clothing such as stiff shoes, cowboy boots, or slippery soles can be restrictive to movement and unsafe. To be free to move, one must dress for movement. Trousers that are too long must come off; dresses that are too full can be tucked in. But how much better to wear clothing that is more appropriate, that will not impede vision while climbing or twisting around the bar. Not only can the body be more sensitive and responsive when appropriately clad, it is also much safer, and therefore the children act with more confidence. So does the teacher.

What other values are part of the culture of the gymnasium? It is obvious to all who have worked with small children that few values will be imparted to them verbally, just as few instructions are. Once in a while, the teacher will have to enforce an unspoken rule about no pushing with not so "friendly persuasion," but on the whole, most of these social values will be acquired informally through observation, imitation, participation, and approval or disapproval. With small children, there will be much learning but little formal teaching. The process of socialization—of taking turns, not bumping each other—is the main vehicle for the transmission of values. In a sense the gymnasium can be likened to a society with few written rules and a guiding role of "The Teacher."

The value of self-directed, self-controlled behavior cannot be underestimated as one of the most important and lasting ones to be inculcated. It implies motor control, which many of these posttoddlers of 2½ are just achieving. Children need both the space and time for practicing controlled movements. Just observe the 3-year-old who speeds belly-bump on a scooter and stops inches from hitting his nose against the wall. Or two 4-year-old friends who make a game of passing each other on the balance beam. When there is *more than enough* equipment to go around, children soon

*From E. B. Castle, *The Teacher* (New York: Oxford University Press, 1970).

learn not to wait in line or jump on top of one another. They will often delight in seeing how close they can come without hitting, which demonstrates that they do value controlled behavior if only to make a game of it.

Two 3½-year-old girls chose to match movements on a set of rings that were hung between two benches. Thus they could swing from one bench to the other and return. They managed to discover all possible combinations of working together: side by side, front to back, facing each other, and cannon fashion—one, then the other. Students of educational gymnastics could scarcely have done better on their first try.

Children often invent and value activities we adults would never think of, and it is during much of this self-initiated behavior that they are learning how to learn. Perhaps we ourselves have not put a high enough value on the acquisition of skilled movement or, for that matter, on learning how to learn skilled movement. As we approach the twenty-first century, with predictions of more leisure and longer life expectancy, we may well wish to take heed of these two values. The recreational skills of good movement are no longer the prerogative of a particular class. But it is definitely not the intent of this author to prepare these children for the future except as the inculcation of values has that effect. That they are more skilled, more responsive, more autonomous 2-, 3-, 4-, or 5-year-olds is objective enough.

However, coupled with the value of self-controlled skill—for as most behavior becomes more controlled, it becomes more skillful—is the value of the enjoyment of moving—the sheer, sensuous sensation of movement. There are ever so many intangible sensations associated with moving, like feeling the wind in your face as you run. Most children like to move, and what is pleasurable they will repeat. Just watch a group of youngsters spin until they are so dizzy they fall down, over and over again. Or roll down an embankment up which they again stagger with the disequilibrium of an inebriate. They are, in fact, more likely to value activity and its concomitant sensations than we are to let them. Admonitions such as "Don't run so fast or you will fall" or "Stop spinning, you make me dizzy," only deter children from enjoying the feeling of speed or the fun of vertigo. Ilinx, the pursuit of vertigo, is a wonderful game.

The major value associated with coming to the gymnasium lies in its opportunity for *strenuous* gross motor activities. The unrestrained, unrestricted movements of young children have an aesthetic quality to be valued as well. One of the major components of any laudable dance or gymnastic move is strength, and this is developed through strenuous and sustained activity. Children are naturally quite strong and graceful if allowed to move freely, and these qualities should be encouraged and cherished.

References

Jerome Bruner, *The Relevance of Education* (New York: W. W. Norton & Co., Inc., 1973).

Newell Kephart and Barbara Godfrey, *Movement Patterns and Motor Education* (New York: Appleton-Century-Crofts, 1969).

A. R. Luria, *The Role of Speech in the Regulation of Normal and Abnormal Behavior* (London: Pergamon Press, 1961).

Clark Moustakas, *The Authentic Teacher: Sensitivity and Awareness in the Classroom* (Cambridge, MA: Howard Doyle Publishing Co., 1972).

Renee Ostler and Peter Kranz, "More Effective Communication Through Understanding Young Children's Behavior." *(Young Children, The Journal of the National Association for the Education of Young Children, 31, 1976).*

Caroline Sinclair, *Movement of the Young Child, Ages Two to Six* (Columbus, OH: Charles E. Merrill Publishing Co., 1973).

Burton White, *The First Three Years of Life* (Englewood Cliffs, N.J.: Prentice-Hall, Inc., 1975).

Ralph Wickstrom, *Fundamental Motor Patterns* (2nd ed.) (Philadelphia: Lea & Febiger, 1977).

9

Personnel

*The effectiveness of our work will, of course,
also depend upon our authenticity
as a feeling person, our cognitive intelligence,
our experience and skills, and our commitment
to the magnificent adventure of learning and teaching.* *

Who should plan and supervise this very special physical activity experience? The major responsibility must lie in the hands of fully qualified teachers of physical education who know children from A to Z and who have an innate respect for what they can do.

However, parents, aides, and playground directors who are astute

*From George Isaac Brown, *Human Teaching for Human Learning: An Introduction to Confluent Education* (New York: Viking Press, 1971). Copyright © 1971 by George Isaac Brown.

99

Significance of motor development
Movement skills and activities to facilitate development

← CHILD DEVELOPMENT →

Apparatus for challenge
Teaching competencies

observers can be and often are trained to assume major responsibility. Similar prerequisites are expected from all who are in charge.

Dr. McGuirk of Surrey University, England, addressing a radio audience, stated that babies are much more sophisticated in their learning than we have given them credit for. He went on to say that mastery, which means control, is most important if the child is to learn. And to learn how to learn, there must be early recognition of the signals, signs, and images for learning that surround the child. How much more children from 2½ to 5 can learn in the gymnasium, we are only just beginning to discover. But what special qualifications must this teacher possess? The word *teacher* is chosen advisedly because coaches, who are often associated with the word *gymnasium*, have more specific, long-term goals that are entirely out of keeping with the *educational, developmental* goals of the teacher. The coach has an eye on the champion; the teacher/parent sees the growing, changing, learning child who is not performing at his or her own developmental level.

Knowledge of Child Development

A thorough knowledge of child development is a basic teaching prerequisite—not merely a nodding acquaintance with theories, relevant as they may be, but a thorough steeping in how children learn, how they acquire language, become socialized, and develop psychologically. Taking courses in child development has its pitfalls; academic courses do not always lead to an understanding about things. A firsthand, working–learning relationship with children such as that enjoyed by baby-sitters, playground directors, or camp counselors is highly recommended to supplement academic study.

And the learning that accrues from siblings, particularly younger ones, is not to be underestimated, although it may not be explicit or obvious to the learner. Having ten younger brothers and sisters, as one of my students had, is tantamount to spending a lifetime immersed in child development. Implicit is being able to get along in a large family, with an understanding of how to be accepted and how to foster children's natural desire to belong. This is the basis of socialized behavior.

Knowledge of the Significance
of Motor Development

It is of utmost importance that the significance and contributions of motor development be thoroughly ingested. More and more importance is being attributed to the relationship of motor development to total development—that is, to the integrated nature of children's development, as scientists and educators study young children. This must be thoroughly understood, and its understanding is predicated on the study of motor development as an area of knowledge: *Why* people move (purposes for movement), *how* people move (products of movement), and *how people learn to move.* This latter area of knowledge has been delineated in the first part of the text.

Motor development, learning to move, depends upon all the sense modalities. The organs of sight, audition, and olfaction (teleoceptors) provide sensory awareness of the external environment. Kindergarten and nursery-school organizers plan very carefully for the discriminating development of two of these three senses in the choice of multicolored, -shaped, and -surfaced playthings. There is also a concern for the development of the skin senses (exteroceptors), which give information about touch, pressure, warmth, cold, and pain. There are rudimentary musical instruments to bang, sand and water tables, clay, dough, and finger paints. Scooters, tricycles, carts, and climbing frames—very common components of the play compound—do contribute to the development of the kinesthetic sense in a meaningful way. But is this enough? Gross motor movements are very much a part of child development at this age, so it is most important to provide specifically for their development.

One of the major underlying principles of growth and development is that it takes time—a long time! Most children do not attain the mature form of basic skills until late elementary school, and the body does not attain its mature stature until the early twenties. The threefold objective of this laboratory playground experience is (1) to give children a variety of gross motor experiences that (2) make demands, for the most part, on the *total* body, with particular focus on the proprioceptive mechanisms, and (3) let them practice.

10

Teacher
Competencies

*The effective teacher of young children needs more
than a body of knowledge, more than techniques and skills.
She needs to "tune in" to the needs of children
and to respond to them.*

This chapter addresses the question of the specific skill competencies the
teacher (of physical education) needs in order to work with children this
age. Many parents, aides, and playground directors are or can be skilled
performers, so this chapter is applicable to them as well as the physical
educator.

*From Evelyn Beyer, *Teaching Young Children*, copyright © 1968 by Western Publishing Co.,
Inc. Reprinted by permission of the Bobbs-Merrill Co., Inc.

Physical Skills

The perennial question confronting programs of professional preparation in physical education centers on "how skilled the teacher should be as a performer." To what level of physical proficiency need the trainee aspire for certification? Countries like Great Britain, Australia, Canada, and New Zealand respond with external examiners who pass or fail candidates on the merits of their performance. Curriculum committees in the United States design courses of study in selected groups of activities, so prospective teachers will have a range of experiences, and lately the notion of proficiency testing has had rather widespread appeal. This latter method may raise more questions than it answers, because entrance qualifications, means of obtaining skills, quantity of skills needed, as well as the proficiency standards and who shall administer them are all part of the problem.

The question of physical skills needed by the teacher has been left until last quite intentionally for the following reasons:

1. There is no categorical answer. The question is almost as much of an enigma as this one: "What skills do you need to become a parent?" Child development specialists state that many young mothers begin intuitively to talk to their babies and thus form the basis of language development. What personal experiences does the beginning physical educator need to begin to work intuitively in the area of motor development? Because the person has run, jumped, and thrown balls since early childhood, and likes to do these things, does this mean that there may be a basis for intuition to operate?

2. Does being able to move well mean that good movement can be taught to or evoked in others? This has been a basic assumption, but what do we know about the relationship between a highly skilled teacher and the skill development of the very young child? We do know that it takes the Muriel Grossfelds and the Bob Beatys to produce Olympic performers, but what about the other end of the spectrum of movement? How skilled a performer must this teacher be?

Jerome Robbins can choreograph a ballet like *West Side Story* without dancing all the parts, because he understands good movement and how dancers learn. It is this author's contention that these are the two important criteria for the teachers under discussion as well. The gymnasium, playground, and backyard are, in effect, where each child will choreograph his or her own movement pattern, where the teacher sets out the equipment for these individual movement sequences to occur. The teacher knows most of the possibilities for movement, because the range of movement of the body is known. After setting the stage, then, the teacher becomes the audience—a very well informed audience, to be sure, but neither a participant nor a model. Here, once again, the analogy of language comes to mind. The nursery-school teacher/parent/aide knows what the word run sounds like and feels like in the mouth and face. Physical educators know what run sounds like both as a word and as a rhythmic pattern of movement, and they know how the body feels when running. Moreover, they know how it feels to run in circles, zigzag, backwards, and even sideways because they have done it. And they know where the eyes must be focused if one is to avoid bumping other people. They can change the speed of the run, its quality, its focus, and its purpose, and they can see when children make all these changes.

Knowledge and sensations of all the fundamental movement patterns will provide beginning teachers and parents with some understanding of how they are performed, why they are performed as they are by young children, and how they can be changed or will be changed by time and practice.

So the fundamental question of performance level of the teacher has been parried. The higher the level of skill attained in gymnastics or dance, the more likely teachers are to encourage a 3-year-old to do a hip circle on the bar or move with grace across the floor. And the more experience the gymnast or dancer has had in choreography, the more likely she or he is to notice movement sequences and see alternative possibilities. A strong background in the theory and practice of movement education and educational gymnastics is urged, since these two subjects lend themselves most naturally to the problem-solving, guided discovery approach that is the basis for this particular, developmental gymnastic experience.

Teaching Skills

The major skill of teaching is communication, the ability to "read" what children 2½ to 5 years old need and to fulfill those needs in a variety of ways. So, above all, these teachers have to keep their eyes and ears open to the lively signals that tell what the children want and are ready to learn. It is easy to see what piece of equipment does not invite them. Not so easy to see how it may be changed to challenge them. Physical education teachers bring to the gymnasium their knowledge and understanding of people in general and of small children in particular—their need for activity, acceptance, and assurance. It is most important that they communicate a belief in the need for a solid foundation of gross motor activity and that they believe they can be instrumental in helping children to achieve it. They must demonstrate by action or expression that they can help children to gain physical skills and confidence in themselves, in their ability to learn, to trust themselves and others. Trust is one of the most basic emotions to be communicated. The way a child places a hand in yours or looks into your eyes indicates trustfulness or fear. Although there are many factors about the gymnasium and the nursery-school room that are not analogous, they do require many of the same attendant skills of teaching. Beyer (1968) has quite a comprehensive list with very sensitive illustrations of what each of these skills means, both to the teacher and the children. Some of her items are repeated here:*

1. Preschool teaching seems more supporting than instructing or informing.
2. Values are caught from one who practices rather than taught by moralizing and threatening.
3. Behavior is described rather than interpreted or analyzed ("You hit Johnny").
4. Children need to be loved and enjoyed by their teacher.
5. They need to be valued and accepted as they are, without blame or judgment for their feelings. (pp. 73-78)

Teachers must be particularly sensitive to these needs of children, but they too have needs that must be communicated.*

1. Since they are in charge, they have a need to be clear and decisive about rules and behavior. This helps them to maintain a learning environment, and it helps children learn to work within specified psychological boundaries.
2. Since they are human beings with feelings, they need to be aware of being tired, annoyed, discouraged. To combat the constant demand for physical strength involved in lifting up a child, pulling two fighters apart, or setting up apparatus, teachers need to have stamina, strength, and resourcefulness.
3. Because they are the authority, there is a need to remain teacherlike rather than childlike in their behavior. This behavior aids the children in developing the concepts of adult and child behavior.
4. One of the wonderful, rejuvenating aspects of working with small children is their freshness, openness, and sense of wonder. Teachers need to be alert, aware, and responsive to this particular aspect of child behavior and recognize it as one of the best sources of psychological refreshment.
5. Teachers need to be full of ideas without imposing them.

*From Evelyn Beyer, *Teaching Young Children*, copyright © 1968 by Western Publishing Co., Inc. Reprinted by permission of the Bobbs-Merrill Co., Inc.

6. Teachers need to have compassion for the troubled and the troublesome; because they are troubled, they are troublesome, both to themselves and to the teacher.

And finally, in Beyer's (1968) words: "Teachers teach attitudes toward
others by their own attitudes of caring, of understanding, of sympathy, of
enjoyment, and approval. They teach by casual demonstration. In their
spontaneous responses to children, they are teaching the attitudes they
hope their children will acquire" (p. 151).* Bruner (1965), too, is particularly relevant in his statement that "our aim as teachers is to give our
students as firm a grasp of a subject as we can, and to make them as
autonomous and self-propelled a thinker as possible" (p. 68).

References

JEROME S. BRUNER, "The Act of Discovery." In Ira Gordon (Ed.), *Human
Development: Readings in Research* (Glenview, IL: Scott, Foresman
and Co., 1965).

*From Evelyn Beyer, *Teaching Young Children*, copyright © 1968 by Western Publishing Co.,
Inc. Reprinted by permission of the Bobbs-Merrill Co., Inc.

Characteristics that attract children's attention:
novelty and changes, the surprising, the incongruous, complexity,
but the largest category . . . is learned. Whatever is significant,
i.e., has previously led to smiles, or is familiar . . .
has a better chance of being noticed than other cues.

PREREQUISITES:

For the Playground,
Backyard, or Gymnasium
Environment

11

The Learning
Environment

*Perhaps more than anything else,
youngsters need to make an impact on their environment;
to get the feel of it . . . to master it.**

Castle (1970), addressing the same element of the learning process, states:
"Restrict the child's desires to the attainable and he will be happy because
he *feels* free" (p. 127).** Of primary concern, then, is that the gymnasium
should be child centered. In essence, this means, first of all, that no piece of
equipment will be placed on the floor unless it is *expected* to be used *freely*

*Reprinted by permission from *Play and Playgrounds* by Jeannette Stone, p. 18. Copyright ©
  1970, National Association for the Education of Young Children, 1834 Connecticut Avenue,
  N.W., Washington, D.C. 20009.
**From E. B. Castle, *The Teacher* (New York: Oxford University Press, 1970).

when the children arrive. One of the first things that strikes their eyes are the ropes, so there should be enough to accommodate a large percent of the children, if not all of them. Conversely, a trampoline is very popular in gymnastic schools because children can bounce on it like so many pieces of popcorn in a popper, with little danger or fear of being hurt, but how many can get on at once? And how many adults does it take to supervise this activity? Where must the teacher's attention be if one is in use? Every piece of equipment must be a possibility for some child to use as he or she wishes, and this means using it unconditionally.

Let us look for a moment at the possible range of developing skills. A tot who is 2½ in September may be a posttoddler and rather unskilled, especially if the child is a boy and he is a little overweight. Conversely, a light-boned, wiry girl of 2½ may, like Shelly, be all over everything with comparative safety. At the other end of the age range, many 4-year-olds are pretty skillful and independent, so the developmental range for any group may be very wide, even within a single age grouping. How do you provide for this?

Quantity is the first consideration, and size may be the first component. Having both large and small equipment is not always a good indicator. When given a choice, most of the children of my acquaintance will choose a sixteen-inch ball instead of a small one and often will go on the tallest, rather than the lowest, piece of apparatus. So "small things (including space) for small tots" can be fallacious reasoning. Because of the range in their developmental level, and possibly an even greater range in their aptitudes and attitudes, dimensional variations are an answer.

As indicated under the section on activities, children should have the choice of jumping from a 2-, 3-, or 4-foot height; balancing on a 2-, 3-, 4-, or 10-inch beam; or climbing a 5-, 8-, or 12-foot ladder. They are the best judges of their own readiness and interest. The angle of inclination of ladders, beams, and slides is another factor to be taken into account. The sensory feedback from walking a horizontal beam is quite different, particularly in the proprioceptors of the ankles and legs, from walking up a steep incline. And children do find delight in running down a slide that many of us might think too steep to negotiate in any way but on the seat. So equipment that can be set out to offer variety in height, width, and angle of inclination provides in part for differing developmental levels and interests.

Different surfaces and colors do this as well. Children with special needs seem to love the feeling of a slippery mat on their bare bellies. We know that the sense of touch remains dominant for a longer time with retarded children than with children who follow a more normal developmental pattern. The tactile sense is one we have only just begun to recognize as important in the gymnasium. But just picture a timid tot balancing

A 2-year-old's jump.

with confidence on a beam whose matting offers traction to her tiny toes. The sensation of the rope on bare hands, feet, and knees; the squeezability of sponge-rubber balls; the freedom of bare feet and bare bodies—all must have a more prominent part in our planning. Interestingly enough, children with special needs are often eager to disrobe while on the apparatus, but it is often difficult to convince the normal child with long trousers to take them off or even roll them up. Such are the rigors of socialization.

Once you become acquainted with a group, it is relatively easy to plan for their specific level of motor skill. As the group progresses from September to June, from 2½ to 3 and from 4 to almost 5, apparatus can be made higher and more challenging; and because they are more dependable and wiser choice makers, it will be comparatively safe. But what is safe within this context?

Was Shelly, at two, safe going over the top of a ten-foot ladder? There are two aspects of safety—physical and psychological—and we must consider both as being equally important. Fear is learned. It is based on knowledge of consequences—either parent instilled or from losing one's grip on a bar and falling, from having someone jump on top of you, or getting in the way of a swing and being knocked over. The child who learns

Up, up, and away—a 4-year-old.

Wings—a 5-year-old.

to avoid such situations after a single accident is fortunate, indeed, but the one who has a permanent sense of apprehension is to be pitied. It is my conviction that very few accidents occur when there is plenty of space, plenty of appropriate equipment, and—perhaps more importantly—an alert, attending adult. It isn't so much the height or kind of apparatus as it is the space around it, the protection offered by mats, and its placement in relation to other pieces. Observe climbing equipment on a playground, and you will notice how much distance there is between pieces. This space itself invites running and predisposes the area to safety.

Planning the approach to the equipment, how to get there, the pathways available, is something children practice from the time they are old enough to escape an inattentive parent: They make a beeline for whatever catches their fancy. There is bound to be a bump as one beeline intersects another, but the bruises are usually incidental to the fun they're having, and they brush themselves off and get on with it. Once in a while, a child may look around to see who is watching and will cry only if someone is. I have operated successfully and safely under the notion that when children have many choices they are the ones who, to paraphrase Castle (1970), restrict their desires to the attainable and so feel free and safe. Once in a while, in September, there is a child who finds it impossible to leave the loving lap of an aide or parent, but never is the child coerced. Who, we may ask, really wants to sit this one out when everyone else is having so much fun? For the most part, when the choices are really the child's, this child is pretty safe both physically and psychologically. The ability to interpret and make sense of the gymnastic equipment is really what determines the "psychological" safety. When children can be their own authorities in matters of choice and still understand that there is an adult to help if help is needed, then they feel free to engage in activities in their own way. Adults do provide emotional security to many children, so they are nice to have around as audience, reinforcer, or helper. "Watch me!" "Did you see what I did?" "Will you help me?" are queries heard most frequently by teachers who are really listening, looking, and responding, three requisites which the child needs and deserves.

It often takes time for children to "sort out" what they know—that is, what looks familiar—and what they don't know—what looks strange—and why. If they have been in a prenursery situation with one slide or if they have one in their own yard, and now there are five slides, this takes an adjustment. They may look for what they are familiar with, as the young baby searches strange faces for that of the mother. I have seen very young children stand looking around for several minutes before setting one foot on the floor. If you watched very closely, you would see that they were participating in the whole experience with their eyes. Thinking, at this age, is still very much tied to actions, and the way they see things with their eyes dominates how they interpret them. So if children cannot find something familiar—that is, something within their experience that they are used to climbing on—the apparatus may be interpreted as unfamiliar and, hence, uninviting. Children ages 2½ to 5 are in Piaget's second stage of development, able to recreate action in their own minds; and most of them, except the very youngest, are able to use symbols, words, to represent these thoughts. They may, therefore, be able to tell you why they stand and look for such a long time. And again, they may not, for they may not know what is scary and unfamiliar or why. This first step into such a wonderful world of activity requires confidence and a feeling of competence to cope with it all; and this is so very personal.

Large Apparatus

It is one thing to purchase equipment with preschool-age children in mind, and it is another thing to utilize what has been designed for older children. Full-sized gymnastic equipment, parallel and uneven bars, Swedish window ladders and box, a horse, buck, or horizontal ladder can be used.

Variety in climbing apparatus.

Whittle equipment like the trestle tree can be purchased. And small equipment such as sawhorses two, three, four feet high can be built and painted bright colors. The challenging aspect is to see how different pieces can be put together for variety, novelty, incongruity, and strangeness and to fit the size and developmental level of the children.

Variety means that children may balance on high or low, level or inclined, balance beams; they may jump from beam, box, or springboard. *Novelty* includes placing a horizontal ladder between two four-foot horses to be used as a bridge one day and, when covered with mats, to be used as a tunnel the next day. *Incongruity* places a slide on each bar of the parallel bars, at opposite ends and in opposite directions. And *strangeness* may simply mean to omit placing mats under the ropes, the ends of which are as high as a small child's nose. Under these conditions the children swing and slice or twist easily on the slippery floor. With two ropes they twist as you and I used to on the playground swings and then untwist with dizzying rapidity. Since they can scarcely do more than hang, twist, or slide, they are rarely in danger of falling.

A ladder tied to a climbing frame permits safe exploration of heights for Razif, age 3.

Parents constructed this cargo net as a training place for a future sailor.

Safety

The following are guidelines for setting up the apparatus.

1. Put out only what children may use *safely*.
2. Decide what pieces of apparatus need to be *matted* and where. A mat placed lengthways away from the apparatus may induce the child to roll following a jump.
3. Consider the *flow* of movement within the entire gymnasium, around each piece of apparatus and from piece to piece. This type of setup is similar to educational gymnastics, in which the participants utilize more than one piece during a particular movement sequence.

Variety

1. Set up the apparatus for those eight movement activities described in the following chapter by preparing for variety within each activity.

Kristofer climbs carefully, using both hands and feet for gripping.

That is, if there are five pieces of equipment from which the children can jump, plan that these are set at differing heights, so the children can have options for jumping.

2. Change the apparatus from day to day, so it presents a different visual picture to the children.

Challenge

Utilize the attributes of novelty, strangeness, and incongruity as much as possible, bearing in mind that what is too novel (climbing on an elephant), too strange (sliding down its trunk), and too incongruous (having the elephant in the gym in the first place) will inhibit movement rather than invite it. This does, however, bring out the fact that children, more than adults, often find more than one use for a particular piece of apparatus. Or they choose to use it differently from the way in which those who set it out thought it might be used. How well I remember the day I set out the Swedish box with an inclined plane attached to it, thinking the children would run up and jump off. Not a bit of it. They climbed on the box and ran down. They have no preconceived notions of how the apparatus *should* be used, but they are quick to see how it *can* be used by them.

Teacher Placement

The teacher must be near the most challenging piece of apparatus, with a clear view of the whole gymnasium, but must be free to wander. Contradictory? No, for there are bound to be other adults, whether parents or aides or students. If there is more than one high piece, for example, place a responsible person next to each one, and be certain that each person faces the entire gym as well. This positioning is critical. The ability to take in almost everything that is going on comes with practice; in fact, the ability to foresee the outcome of a child's action develops rather rapidly if one looks with this in mind. The 2½-year-old who makes a beeline toward something with no thought of the swinging child in between may have to be snatched in a hurry from the oncoming body. There is no possible way to avoid all collisions, nor would you want to; but it is imperative that no one be so badly hurt that the experience becomes traumatic. Children are infinitely resilient, but we want to keep them that way so that they will want, more than anything else, to return to the gymnasium.

Some of the physical education books for Infant Schools in England have setups for the gymnasium that include many ideas that can be incorporated. (Note: The term *infant*, in the United States, applies to the pretoddler, the period prior to the onset of walking. The British use the term as roughly comparable to American lower elementary-school grades, however.) Many of the author's ideas grew out of her experience in teaching educational gymnastics both to elementary-school children and college students in the United States and in England.

12

Movement Activities

*There exists a general lack of attention
to the kinds of quality of movement experiences
which are a part of the preschool child's life—
that crucial developmental period from birth to age five or six.
Such neglect stems from the belief
that the child's movement responses develop "naturally,"
presumably as the result of some inner clock-like mechanism.**

The following activities that children love and that also contribute to
components of motor development such as strength, cardiovascular endurance, coordination, and agility are discussed: balancing, climbing,
hanging, jumping, running, sliding, spinning, and swinging. This list
differs from that delineated by Andrews, who has a well-chosen concern
for locomotor and nonlocomotor dichotomy. There is some overlap with

*Valerie Hunt, Jeanne Grenzeback, and B. Egle, *Movement Education for Pre-School Pro-
grams* (St. Ann, MO: Cemrel, Inc., National Program on Early Childhood Education, 1972),
p. 3.

the excellent depiction of fundamental motor patterns of Wickstrom, and it is more detailed than that which Hunt presents. This section is concerned with those activities that challenge young children and make major contributions—physical, physiological, and psychological—to their motor development. This stance does not negate the importance of the kinds of specific skills that Andrews, Wickstrom, and Sinclair address. It is this author's belief that the selected activities contribute more to a generalized pool of sensory-motor experiences that form a base from which specific skills emerge. The larger and more diversified the base, the greater the selection the child has to draw from. As with language, the number and variety of words form the basis for sentence structure, complexity, and comprehensibility. Young children are acquiring a vocabulary of movement that includes the basic locomotor skills of running, sliding, skipping, and hopping; the nonlocomotor or axial forms of twisting, bending, and stretching; the fundamental motor patterns of catching, kicking, and striking. But they are doing more.

These activities may be compared to children's diet, which should always include the nutritional basics: protein, fats, carbohydrate, minerals, and vitamins.

Protein	Fat
Minerals/Vitamins	Carbohydrate

Square Meal

During this physiologically impressionable stage of children's lives, adequate protein—the body-building component—is vital, but the other nutrients determine its utilization. Large muscle activity is comparable to the protein ingredient. It is *the* ingredient largely responsible for integrated body development. Children become apathetic, remain small, and become incapable of movement without an adequate amount of large muscle activity. And what is adequate? Doctors say that from three to five hours daily of strenuous activity is good insurance of development for elementary-school children; presumably, it would be considerably less for the preschool-age child. Let us consider the specific activity, equipment that provides for it, and the contributions it makes to motor development.

ACTIVITY	EQUIPMENT	CONTRIBUTION
Balancing	balance beams 3″, 4″, 6″, 8″ in width	Proprioceptive mechanism input
	2′–4′ in height Level and inclined	Opposition of limbs Total body assembly
	Scooters and large balls	Vestibular mechanism input

Children are able to walk when functional equilibrium has been developed. This is dependent upon strength of the postural muscles, adequate antigravity reflexes, and development of the proprioceptive— that is, vestibular and kinesthetic—mechanisms, particularly in the lower extremities of the ankles, which are responsive to the demands of upright locomotion. Various activities make varying demands on these three components. The hop, one foot to the same foot, is one of the most difficult

David, age 3, chooses to cross the balance beam on his belly.

"Follow the Leader" is a favorite game almost anywhere.

Razif, age 3, crosses carefully. Note the concentration as he places his feet on this homemade balance beam. A 2-inch by 4-inch by 10-foot beam on a sawhorse 1 foot high provides good practice in balancing.

The decision process is involved in deciding to jump when halfway across the balance beam.

skills for young children to accomplish, because the single leg has to have strength enough to propel the weight of the entire body upward and absorb the weight on landing without losing balance. The hop is, in a sense, an indicator of the neuromuscular development of the child, for it reveals the degree to which the inferior or distal portion of the body has matured. Balancing—whether walking a single line, running, or walking a balance beam—makes demands on the neuromuscular, proprioceptive, and vestibular mechanisms. And since balance, or equilibrium, is probably the single most important component of skilled performance, there should be ample opportunity for children to engage in activities that promote it.

ACTIVITY	EQUIPMENT	CONTRIBUTION
Climbing	Ladders	Kinesthesis
	Climbing frames	Total body assembly
	Horse	Opposition of limbs
	Swedish box	Rhythm
	Swedish window ladder	Agility
	Stairs	
	Cargo net	
	Ropes	

Climbing is one of the most challenging activities for young children, beginning even before they can walk, as most mothers of infants well know. The author observed several infants who were able to climb up a small slide, on the slide side, using the same hand–foot pattern as in creeping but with fully extended legs. They were able to grip the rail on either side, and their bare feet adhered safely to the surface. A problem arose when the 12-month-old reached the top and was unable to turn around. Climbing up and climbing down present two extremely different visual problems involving the perception of distance and depth. One has only to approach a flight of stairs from the bottom and from the top to be aware of this. So climbing up, as a skill, precedes climbing down.

The rungs of a ladder and the horizontal parts of a climbing frame must be sufficiently small that tiny fingers and feet can have a firm grip. In order to climb with maximum safety, children should grip with the thumb in opposition rather than alongside the fingers. It is not, however, a corollary that equipment be firm; indeed, wiggly, semistable pieces often are more tempting than something that is firmly fixed. Remember what fun it was to bounce on that newly felled tree?

The cautious climber of 3.

Climbing demands strength, particularly of the arms and upper part of the body; like running, it provides practice in alternation of the right and left arms. It also depends upon opposition of the right arm with the left leg. Few if any children under 5 have either the strength in the hands and arms or the coordination to climb a rope. However, in Australia, where cargo nets and vertical ropes are part of the outdoor equipment at several nursery schools the author visited, the children ascended and descended with ease. Infant schools in England often have a horizontal rope on which children can traverse from one point to another, monkeylike, using their knees or legs instead of their feet. This is a popular way to negotiate the underside of a horizontal ladder that is not too far from the floor.

Ladders are particularly versatile. They may be set at any angle or inclination, from horizontal to vertical, and they permit climbing on rungs or sides via hands and feet or feet alone. Children travel along them in several directions—forward, backward, sideways, on top, or hanging under. Spaces may be dropped through or negotiated in other ways. When placed against uneven parallel bars, for example, they make a rather large, almost formidable, piece of apparatus which the child can negotiate without help from an adult.

The competent climber of 4. Simple equipment like this offers variations in height.

ACTIVITY	EQUIPMENT	CONTRIBUTION
Hanging and Swinging	Ropes	Strength
	Horizontal bars	Proprioceptive input
	Rings	Vestibular input
	Ladders	Orientation in space

Swinging of the body almost invariably accompanies hanging as young children choose to perform it. One has only to witness the use made of the restraining bars at a supermarket to note how often waiting children hang, swing, and turn. They can easily support themselves for astonishingly long periods when hanging by their hands; and since they invariably bring their knees up to their chests, the activity is excellent to develop abdominal strength at a time when their side profiles are just beginning to lose the "Pooh Bear" image of a bulging belly.

Children are innately partial to moving apparatus, so ropes and rings are favorites. The bodily demands of swinging and inverted hanging are monitored by the vestibular, proprioceptive, and neuromuscular mechanisms with feedback that is both very important and different from that of other activities. Inversion of the body is not always a comfortable

Dougy shows different ways of hanging.

When climbing, the sky's the limit.

position for some children, particularly if their eyesight is defective in the least. But it may be considered a lead-up activity to rolling, headstands, and handstands, so voluntary participation is to be encouraged. "You look funny upside down," they say. The feeling of weightlessness in swinging, that of vertigo in twisting on the rope, and that of blood rushing to the head in hanging by the knees are all different sensory experiences that heighten the child's awareness of the body in space.

Swings can be made from many things. Swinging is still "the pleasantest thing ever a child could do."

"Climb aboard, matey!"

A playground launching pad.

Muscles of arm and abdomen are used in this kind of pull-up.

ACTIVITY	EQUIPMENT	CONTRIBUTION
Jumping	Balance beam	Strength
	Horse	Equilibrium
	Swedish box	Proprioceptive input
	Springboard	Vestibular input
		Agility
		Total body assembly

Jumping usually commences with a large step down. It then progresses to the stage of jumping with two feet to landing on both feet, whether down from something, over obstacles, and across things such as a line or an imaginary brook. In all probability, it demands a quicker coordination than any other activity, because the body is defying gravity and then having to cope with it. It certainly gives children a great deal of pleasure to jump, jump and fall, jump and roll, or twist and turn. Such stunting variations are seldom seen in any other activity, and it has been the author's experience that the jump down is highly developed in most children by the age of 4. Many of them will jump from a distance equal to their height, and adventuresome children will drop nearly twice their height. One small 3-year-old girl took particular delight in dropping from and reclimbing the uneven bars for minutes on end. How well I remember a 6-year-old girl who spent the entire thirty minutes of her gym period running up a springboard and doing a somersault onto a ten-inch crash pad. Over and over again.

And then there was Amy. At 3, she was scarcely as tall as the balance beam she crossed unflinchingly time after time. At its end she would jump onto the mat and do a succession of forward rolls across the floor—five, six, or even ten before she would repeat the entire movement sequence. At 4 she seldom rolled.

Skippy, going from a low height to a high one.

Some 3- and 4-year-olds can somersault from a springboard, but it is not a skill one would expect them to learn, since it involves some highly developed skill in inhibiting the "righting reflex."

ACTIVITY	EQUIPMENT	CONTRIBUTION
Running	Space	Cardiovascular endurance
		Total body assembly
		Rhythm
		Agility
		Opposition and alternation of arms and legs

Many 2½-year-olds are still performing a fast walk rather than a true run in which there is a period of nonsupport of the body. The run appears when there is strength enough to propel the body off the floor from a single leg. Children need to develop this strength by running; they also need to practice variations of the run such as running backward, sideways, or in circles. But they need time to learn to stop and to change directions, to accelerate and decelerate. They enjoy running fast, dodging, running on tiptoes, up and down inclined planes, chasing, and being chased. Since running is the basic skill of most of our sports, to run fast becomes a highly prized attainment, and even the smallest children will try to best each other from time to time: "I can run faster than you can." In a sense, running gives children a feeling of freedom. They can move fast enough to escape an overprotective or solicitous parent; they can dodge to safety; they can catch a prize; they can be first and win at many games. Running, like swimming, is a good all-round activity, for it utilizes most of the important postural muscles of the body and contributes to cardiovascular endurance.

ACTIVITY	EQUIPMENT	CONTRIBUTION
Sliding	Inclined benches	Proprioceptors
	Scooters	Vestibular input
	Ropes and poles	

Even the smallest hill is a challenge for most children to run or slide down. The feeling of speed, of self-generated motion, of giving in to gravity must feel good to them, for they engage in it so readily. Nursery schools in the North capitalize on the advent of snow to use flying saucers, sleds, or slippery snowsuits to introduce those who have not already been lucky enough to come in contact with a banister or supermarket railing that invites such activity. Older, more enterprising youngsters resort to the seat of their trousers, cardboard, or trays if they don't own sleds or saucers. The popularity of tiny-tot ski and skating classes addresses the popularity of gliding or sliding on slippery surfaces.

Continuous activity. "So many things to do—climb, slide, and jump."

I met a youngster at the bottom of a slalom course at 9 A.M. one day, just as he snapped his fingers at what looked to me like a feeling of disgust. "What is the matter?" I asked. "I missed a gate," he said.

Q. "How old are you?"

A. "Thix."

Q. "How long have you been skiing?"

A. "Three years."

At 3 P.M. he was still there in his racing helmet.

Q. "Have you missed any gates lately?"

A. "Nooooooo" came to my ear as he whizzed past.

Provision for sliding can be made in the gymnasium in at least four ways: with mats, slides, ropes or poles, and scooters. Of course, a good clean gym floor will encourage the onset of a slide similar to that used in stealing bases at a later age, and boys, particularly, are fond of practicing this. It is, however, one of the "incidental" skills they invent themselves and not usually one that the teacher predetermines.

When mats are placed over, instead of under, the balance beam, for example, children will slide on most any part of their anatomy; and the greater the pig-pile at the bottom, the more giggles it creates. So this, plus sliding down slides, ropes, or poles, is structured into the program. There is, at present, no way of monitoring the vestibular and proprioceptive feedback that accompanies acceleration and deceleration of the body in the slide. Nor do we have concrete evidence of the contribution that sliding makes to neuromuscular development, but we make an educated guess that there is facilitation of development of the proprioceptive mechanism and, as a result, enhancement of body position in space. We do know that these sensations are important to heightened sensory awareness, for astronauts are subjected to similar speed-stalling techniques in their program. The age from 2½ to 5 is particularly important because children's actions and movements are becoming more refined and coordinated in this period, and improved coordination is dependent on more accurate, more immediate, and more sensitive feedback of both an intrinsic and extrinsic nature.

Sliding belly-bump on scooters is a similar situation. The younger ones will usually sit on the scooter and propel themselves with their feet, whereas older ones pick the scooter up and generate a good bit of running speed before landing on it and gliding across the floor. There are, in fact, three rather distinct stages: (1) sit and "hitch," very much as the seat-bottom creeper; (2) lie down and use the hands in alternating fashion, much as in swimming; (3) run and get aboard. The body extension these latter groups achieve is something to delight the most demanding gymnast or dancer. The whole body is extended in space in a most beautiful way for both boys and girls. And when one realizes how difficult extension is to

(a)   (b)

Optimal teaching environment: (a) "Can you jump?" (b) "Who can climb, and who can jump?"

"teach" at a later age, the full value of this activity is driven home. Most certainly, they are learning about the use of the body in space.

Another popular activity on scooters and ropes is spinning. Children will often request that you spin them. Incoming signals derived during this activity from the centrifugal action on the semicircular canals of the ear must be translated by the nervous system and then converted into perceptions. The two perceptions that are important are those of body position (segments, especially the head) and speed. Information about these perceptions comes as well from the proprioceptors, with very different sensations being felt on the right and left sides of the body.

The cumulative effect of these activities is one of enhanced development of the neuromuscular, proprioceptive, and vestibular mechanisms, which are responsible for effective, efficient, and expressive motor control. As Ridenour (1978) reports, there is research currently underway studying perceptual characteristics and movement organization, which ultimately can supply even more information for the designing of "optimal teaching environments for developmental movement activities" (p. 26).

Behaviors to Discourage

1. *Showing off.* The show-off usually needs an audience, so move away.
2. *Going higher.* Competition may force a child to go higher than he or she would if alone.
3. *Shouting and/or noise in general.* This is a very individual thing. Some teachers' threshold for noise is very high, but children do not need to shout to have fun. Happy, laughterlike noise is wonderful and an almost necessary adjunct to enjoyment.
4. *Pushing.* Pushing and pulling are healthy, normal activities that, with careful planning, can be structured into a program. With sufficient equipment, there is little need to push in order to be first, so selective planning can obviate much of the need to push. Taking turns is an important concept to learn.
5. *Power struggle.* Socially acceptable behavior is rather easy to enforce in the context of the gymnasium because the activities are so popular. A showdown of any kind, between child and child or teacher and child, is to be avoided. The only example that comes to mind is one in which a child did not choose to take off his shoes. He was permitted to participate with his shoes on, and the next time he came, it was no issue for him; he took his shoes off of his own accord.

Note: Although the trampoline may contribute to motor development, and certainly ranks high on the scale of things young children like, its use for regular gymnasium experiences is doubtful or questionable. Small children bounce like popcorn while all the others stand and watch. There seem to be two factors that are antithetical to good gymnasium management: (1) The teacher can watch only one piece of equipment at a time, and a trampoline has to be monitored every minute it is in use; and (2) children have to stand and wait. Perhaps the place for trampolines is in the private studio.

> *Man seems to prefer to learn creatively, by exploring,*
> *questioning, experimenting, testing,*
> *and modifying ideas and solutions.*
>
> E. PAUL TORRANCE (1962)*

*From E. Paul Torrance, *Guiding Creative Talent* (Huntington, N.Y.: Robert E. Krieger Publishing Co., 1976). Reprinted with permission of the author and publisher.

In conclusion, the idea is to provide an environment that fosters independence; individuality, the opportunity for decision making, experimentation, and divergent thinking; and that is both physically and psychologically safe.

Behaviors to Encourage

1. *Variety of movements.* "Can you skip?" "Can you hop on or over that line?" "Can you run fast and then slow down?" "Can you run forward, backward, and zigzag?"
2. *Working together, socializing, taking turns.* "Can you find a way to jump with John, or jump over him?"
3. *Imitating other children's movement.* "See how Susie jumped. Can you do it?"
4. *Being different.* "Bob's legs were together when he jumped. Can you find a different way to stretch your legs when jumping?"
5. *Good body alignment.* "Your body is so straight when you glide on the scooter."
6. *A sequence of movements.* "Can you run, jump, and then roll?"
7. *Curiosity, inquiry.* "How many ways can you twist your body when you are on the rings?"
8. *Creativity.* "I saw you twisting as you ran. What other movements can you do as you run?"
9. *Verbalization, especially making sentences.* "What color ball would you like? Can you say that you would like a yellow one?"
10. *Decision making.* "Which piece of apparatus would you like to go on first?"

References

MARCELLA V. RIDENOUR (Ed.), *Motor Development: Issues and Applications* (Princeton, N.J.: Princeton Book Company, 1978).

13

Developmental
Activities

Content without process is blind;
process without content is empty. *

A whole host of activities can be built around the simple locomotor and
nonlocomotor words, prepositions, numbers, body parts, body shapes, and
elements of space. The way in which teachers and parents choose to
structure experiences by verbal instruction is determined by the children's
responsiveness and their own imagination. There are days when the

*From Itty Chan, *Observing Children, A Science, Working with Them, An Art.* Reprinted by
permission from *Young Children,* vol. 33, no. 2 (Jan. 1978), p. 61. Copyright © 1978, National
Association for the Education of Young Children, 1834 Connecticut Avenue, N.W., Washington, D.C. 20009.

equipment itself is so exciting that to infringe upon their freedom to explore is sacrilege. There are other days when the children are particularly responsive to verbal prompting. *Locomotor words* are some of the first ones they learn:

		NONLOCOMOTOR WORDS	
walk	slide		
run	gallop	twist	spin
hop	crawl	turn	curl
skip	creep	bend	balance
jump	roll	stretch	rock

CHILD-INSPIRED WORDS

wiggle	shake	bang
squiggle	burst	pop
squirm	swoosh	bounce

PREPOSITIONS		ORDINAL AND CARDINAL NUMBERS	
on	through	one	twice, etc.
off	around	two, etc.	first
over	along	once	second, etc.
under	about		
into			

BODY PARTS	BODY SHAPES	SPACE ELEMENTS
hand	straight	directions
foot, feet	angular, crooked	pathways
head	curled, round	levels
hips	twisted	
back	flat	
shoulders		

Teacher directions begin very simply: "*Walk on* the white line [jump rope, string]." "*Hop over* the blue line [stone, stick, leaf, ball]." The combination of words is almost infinite and helps children to recognize and use them. "*Wiggle under* the balance beam [ladder, wire]." This may be individualized by having all the 4-year-olds—with their own stick, stone, leaf, or shoe—find a way to go over or around it. "Now make it go over [around, through] you." Children themselves can be obstacles to be gone over, around, or through, and this becomes a very challenging activity as they make front and back bridges or wide shapes. And as they learn to listen to and follow directions, the tasks can become more complicated: "*Walk on* the white line; then *hop over* the blue one." "*Wiggle under* the balance beam; then *go over* it using your hands."

The degree of complication of these tasks will be determined by the age range of the children—their experiences as well as the individual ages. Children 2½ years old may imitate but not understand, whereas 4- and 5-year-olds are capable of following a rather long sequence: "Go *across* the climber, *down* the slide headfirst, and *along* the beam sideways." Since many 5-year-olds can identify letters and write, a blackboard or card with the word on it makes quite a game of it.

Balancing is a favorite activity that utilizes various body parts. "Can you balance on one hand and one foot?" "On a knee and the head?" Children will think up their own combinations, becoming quite specific, with right and left included as qualifying the part or side of the body.

Body shapes add yet another dimension to the variety of activities. Children love to be picked up as a test of how tightly curled or stiff their bodies are. It is a wonderful game of "me next" of which the teacher often tires before the children. The concept of opposition—straight–crooked, thin–wide—can be developed here as well: "How wide can you make your body?"

Taking cues from educational gymnastics, the gym can be set up more or less for one specific theme or activity, such as body shapes or jumping. In the latter, the focus can be on learning to jump from, over, across, or onto equipment. Two 4-in. by 4-in. by 12-in. boards with a notch on top will hold a wand or stick and make a good hurdle. These, set in series, help develop the rhythm necessary for the specific sport skill, and children love to practice this particular activity. Obstacles such as a low balance beam or rope are easily jumped over. A springboard elicits jumps for height followed in many cases by a roll and in some by a dive roll. Learning to jump and roll is an excellent safety skill. Any teacher working with young children would do well to become steeped in knowledge of educational gymnastics, which foster a much less stereotypical movement than Olympic gymnastics.

And when music is added to the foregoing, it becomes like a game of "Statues"—the intent of which is not to be caught moving and to make a good shape. Once attending skills are rather well developed (and to further enhance their development), children respond to simple directions like these: "Move around the room [hop, skip, run, jump] as long as you hear the music. When it stops, make a round shape on some piece of equipment." "Next time make a shape with your feet higher than your head." "Balance on one foot and one hand." The more difficult the challenge, the better the response. The fun of the whole game is being caught in an upside-down position while on a swinging rope or the top of a trestle tree. The game element of being caught is a very inviting challenge for children. And combining music and apparatus is particularly exciting. The music itself will help determine the movements. Many children of this age can distinguish instrumental voices, as in *Peter and the Wolf*, and changes in tempo, as in *The Nutcracker Suite*, and they can move accordingly.

Words themselves can be an inducement to movement. "Show me a *whoosh* [*blast-off, bang, pop, sizzle*]." And quite a variety of sounds can be produced on a tambourine either by the teacher or children.

The addition of balls of different kinds, sizes, shapes, and colors and of bean bags provides another dimension. Practice in rolling a ball under any piece of equipment, or tossing it over, gives practice in retrieval as well. We know that young children can track the movement of an object, but they need to learn to move their bodies into position to collect or intercept it. So a window ladder becomes something to throw through, a slide to roll the ball up or down, a swinging rope a target to hit, or a stool to dribble around with feet or hands. Suggestions, rather than formal instruction, are in order now: "Can you roll the ball under the trestle tree and go catch it?" Children will often find their own challenges such as rolling a ball under a hurdle and jumping over it. The astute teacher picks up and uses these child-inspired ideas.

Hippity-hop balls provide an unusual opportunity for the develop-

Balance, coordination, and strength are required and developed when riding this hippity-hop ball.

The twister gives this 4-year-old incentive to practice the nonlocomotor body actions that involve almost all the joints of the body.

ment of coordination, balance, and strength. And children are challenged to race, maneuver through obstacle courses, and investigate the possibility of going safely up and off a low-inclined plane. They will repeat many of the same challenges on gym scooters, finding equipment to squeeze under, go around, or—as with the inclined plane—slide down. Total body extension is developed on these as in no other aspect of the gymnasium. Spinning, going fast, and stopping suddenly are all fun things to do and are usually self-initiated.

Climbing Apparatus

The concept of a knotted rope hanging from a beam in the ceiling of a gymnasium or classroom, from a swing frame as in the illustration on page 148, or from a specially-designed frame or tree is a winner because the ropes move. Children love moving things. Ropes can be purchased from a hardware store and a parent or teacher can knot and fasten them with little difficulty. If there is plenty of space available a tire may be included either in a vertical plane as is so often seen in the backyard, or in a horizontal plane. The latter permits two or more children to utilize it simultaneously. It then becomes a pirate ship, an aircraft in a bumpy sky, or a spinning top. The cargo net is another rope formation which challenges most children to climb.

The Versatile Saw Horse

The saw horse pictured below is most versatile and easily constructed. Ones of varying heights (2 feet, 3 feet, and 4 feet) can be used alone, as this one is, or connected by the board to make a balance beam or a series of beams to be negotiated. A board 2 inches by 8 inches by 10 feet is sufficiently sturdy for five-year-olds, but it must have a lip on one or both ends to fasten over the horse. The lip is a board 2 inches by 2 inches by 8 inches attached to the very end of the long board. When horses like this are painted bright colors, it adds to the directions a teacher may give: "Tommy, put the yellow beam on the blue horse." "Go over the red beam, crawl under the green horse, and walk along the yellow beam." This equipment is light enough for the children to handle so they can set up their own gym apparatus.

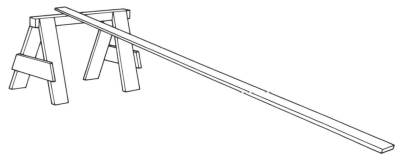

Slide

Broad slides offer multiple options to children, and the wide ladder permits more than one child to climb at a time. Sharing is most important at this age and its concept is easily included with equipment like this.

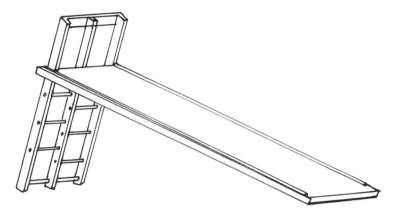

Climbing Frame

Perhaps the most versatile piece of apparatus is this climbing frame. Ladders and beams can be attached to its rungs in an infinite number of ways. Its legs are 4 inches by 4 inches by 4 feet. The connecting crosspieces may be either of wood or metal so the frame will be very sturdy and can hold several children at a time. When two bars cross the top the long way children can hang as well as climb.

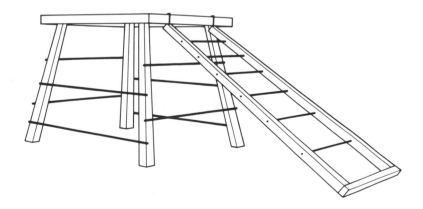

These four pieces of apparatus provide for all of the major body activities: hanging, climbing, swinging, jumping, balancing, and sliding, and, when used in conjunction with each other, provide an infinite variety of options for children to follow.

Appendix

Additional
References

Preface

LOLAS HALVERSON, "Development of Motor Patterns in Young Children"
(Quest VI, A Symposium on Motor Learning 6, 1966).

JEAN PIAGET, "Mastery Play." In J.S. Bruner and others (Ed.), *Play* (New York:
Penguin, 1951).

CAROLINE SINCLAIR, *Movement for the Young Child Ages Two to Six* (Columbus, OH: Charles E. Merrill, 1973).

KATHY SYLVA, JEROME S. BRUNER, and PAUL GENOVA, in J. S. Bruner, et. al. (Ed.), *Play: Its Role in Development and Evolution* (New York: Basic Books, 1976).

Chapter 2

AAHPER Convention (Berkeley, CA: The Regents of the University of California, 1971).

PAUL M. FITTS and M. POSNER, *Human Performance* (Belmont, CA: Brooks/ Cole Publishing Company, 1967).

BETTY FLINCHUM, *Motor Development in Early Childhood; A Guide for Movement Education with Ages 2–6* (St. Louis, MO; C.V. Mosby Co., 1975).

ARNOLD GESELL, FRANCES L. ILG, and LOUISE BATES AMES, *Infant and Child in the Culture of Today* (New York: Harper & Row, 1974).

LOLAS HALVERSON, "Development of Motor Patterns in Young Children" (Quest VI, a Symposium on Motor Learning 6, 1966).

HUGH PERKINS, *Human Development and Learning* (2nd ed.), Institute for Child Study, University of Maryland (Belmont, CA: Wadsworth Publishing Co., 1974).

G. LAWRENCE RARICK, *Physical Activity, Human Growth and Development* (New York: Academic Press, 1973).

MARY SHERIDAN, *Children's Developmental Progress From Birth to Five Years: The Stycar Sequences* (Windsor, Berks, England: NFER Publishing Co., Ltd., 1977).

CAROLINE SINCLAIR, *Movement for the Young Child Ages Two to Six* (Columbus, OH: Charles E. Merrill, 1973).

JERRY THOMAS and PETER BENDER, "A Developmental Explanation for Children's Motor Behavior: A Neo-Piagetian Interpretation." In Daniel Landers and Robert Christina (Eds.), *Psychology of Motor Behavior and Sport,* Vol. II (University Park, PA: The Pennsylvania State University, 1976).

RICHARD WALKER, "Body Build and Behavior in Young Children," *Body-Build and Nursery School Teacher's Ratings, Monograph of the Society for Research in Child Development* (New Haven: Gesell Institute of Child Development, 3, 1952), pp. 27–84.

JOSEPH P. WINNICK, *Early Movement Experiences and Development; Habilitation and Remediation* (Philadelphia: W.B. Saunders Company, 1979).

Chapter 3

A. JEAN AYERS, *Sensory Integration and Learning Disorders* (Los Angeles, CA: Western Psychological Services, 1977).

J.V. Basmajian, *Muscles Alive* (Baltimore, MD: Williams & Wilkins Co., 1974).

Virginia Bell, *Sensorimotor Learning from Research to Teaching* (Pacific Palisades, CA: Goodyear Publishing Company, Inc., 1970).

Hugh Brown, *Brain and Behavior* (New York: Oxford University Press Inc., 1976).

Aren Carlsten and Gunnar Grimby, *The Circulatory Response to Muscular Exercise in Man* (American Lecture Series in Sports-medicine), (Springfield, IL: Charles C. Thomas, 1966).

John Dickinson, *Proprioceptive Control of Human Movement* (Princeton, N.J.: Princeton Book Company, 1976).

John Eccles, *Understanding the Brain*, (New York: McGraw-Hill, 1973).

Edward V. Evarts, *Brain Mechanisms in Movement* (Scientific American Offprints) (San Francisco, CA: W. H. Freeman and Co., July 1973).

Anita Harrow, *A Taxonomy of the Psychomotor Domain* (New York: David McKay Co., 1972).

Joseph Higgins, *Human Movement: An Integrated Approach* (St. Louis, MO: C.V. Mosby Company, 1977).

Ronald Marteniuk, *Information Processing in Motor Skills* (New York: Holt, Rinehart & Winston, 1976).

P.A. Merton, "How We Control the Contraction of Our Muscles" (*Scientific American*, Vol 226, No. 5, May 1972, pp. 30–37).

George Sage, *Introduction to Motor Learning: A Neuropsychological Approach* (Reading, MA: Addison-Wesley Publishing Co., 1971).

Brian Sharkey, *Physiology and Physical Activity* (New York: Harper & Row, 1975).

George Stelmach (Ed.), *Motor Control: Issues and Trends* (New York: Academic Press, 1976).

Chapter 5

Seymour Fisher and Sidney E. Cleveland, *Body Image and Personality* (New York: Dover Publications, Inc., 1968).

Chapter 6

Millie Almy, *Early Childhood Play* (New York: Harper & Row, 1968).

Marian H. Anderson, Margaret E. Elliot, and Jeanne La Berge, *Play with a Purpose* (New York: Harper & Row, 1966).

A. Bengtsson, *The Child's Right to Play* (Sheffield, England: International Playground Association, 1974).

JOAN CASS, *The Significance of Children's Play* (London: B.T. Batsford, Ltd., 1971).

ROBERTA COLLARD, "Exploration and Play in Human Infants" (Washington, D.C.: AAHPER, *Leisure Today*, 1972).

M.J. ELLIS, *Why People Play* (Englewood Cliffs, N.J.: Prentice-Hall, 1973).

LAWRENCE FRANK, *Play Is Valid* (Washington, D.C.: Association for Childhood Education International, 1968).

G. M. GOLDWORTH, *Why Nursery Schools* (Letchworth, Hertfordshire, England: The Garden City Press Limited, 1971).

R. E. HERON & BRIAN SUTTON-SMITH, *Child's Play* (New York: John Wiley & Sons, Inc., 1971).

LADY ALLEN HURTWOOD, M. FLEKKOY, J. SIGSGAARD, and A. SKARD (Eds.), *Space for Play* (Copenhagen: World Organization for Early Childhood Education [OMEP], 1964).

K. JAMESON and P. KIDD, *Pre-School Play* (London: Cassell & Collier Macmillan Pub., Ltd., 1974).

MICHAEL LEWIS, "Sex Differences in Play Behavior of the Very Young" (Washington, D.C.: AAHPER, *Leisure Today*, 1972).

J. MCLELLAN, *The Question of Play* (New York: Pergamon Press, 1970).

Play: The Child Strives Toward Self-Realization, Conference Proceedings (Washington, D.C.: National Association for The Education of Young Children, 1975).

Play: Learning How To (Quest Monograph 26) (Brattleboro, VT: The National Association for Physical Education of College Women, The International Association for Physical Education of College Men, Summer 1976).

DARYL SIEDENTOP, *Physical Education; Introductory Analysis* (Dubuque, IA: Wm. C. Brown Co., 1972).

JEANNETTE STONE, *Play and Playgrounds* (Washington, D.C.: National Association for the Education of Young Children, 1970).

BRIAN SUTTON-SMITH (Ed.), "Research and Thought about Children's Play" (Washington, D.C.: AAHPER, *Leisure Today*, 1972).

Chapter 10

MILLIE ALMY, *Ways of Studying Children; A Manual for Teachers*, (New York: Columbia University, 1959).

MILLIE ALMY, EDWARD CHITTENDEN, and PAULA MILLER, *Young Children's Thinking* (New York: Columbia University, 1966).

Association for Childhood Education International, *Children's Views of Themselves*, Washington, D.C., 1959.

Lois Berman, "More than Choice" *(Educational Leadership, Journal of the Association for Supervision and Curriculum Development 35, no. 6, March 1978, 424–429.*

E. Jeremiah W. Canning, *Values in an Age of Confrontation* (Columbus, OH: Charles E. Merrill, 1970).

Itty Chan, *Observing Young Children, A Science, Working with Them, an Art. Young Children* (Washington, D.C.: National Association for the Education of Young Children, January 1978).

Dorothy Cohen, *The Learning Child* (New York: Pantheon Books, 1972).

Arthur Costa, "Affective Education: The State of the Art," *(Educational Leadership, Journal of the Association for Supervision and Curriculum Development,* January 1977, p. 260).

Richard Curwin and Barbara Fuhrmann, *Discovering Your Teaching Self* (Englewood Cliffs, N.J.: Prentice-Hall, 1975).

Martha Davis, *Understanding Body Movement: An Annotated Bibliography* (New York: Arno Press, 1972).

Mary Carol Day and Roland K. Parker, *The Pre-School in Action: Exploring Early Childhood Programs* (2nd ed.) (Boston: Allyn & Bacon Inc., 1977).

Department of Education and Science, *Movement, Physical Education in the Primary Years* (London: Her Majesty's Stationery Office, 1972).

John Eliot and Neil Salking, *Children's Spatial Development* (Springfield, IL: Charles C. Thomas, 1975).

Ellis Evans, *Contemporary Influences in Early Childhood Education* (Early Childhood Education Series) (New York: Holt, Rinehart & Winston, Inc., 1971).

Hazel Francis, *Language in Childhood* (London: Paul Elek, 1975).

Friedrich Froebel, *The Education of Man* (New York: Appleton-Century-Crofts, 1970).

Lydia Gerhardt, *Moving and Knowing* (Englewood Cliffs, N.J.: Prentice-Hall, Inc., 1973).

Anne Gilbert, *Teaching the Three R's Through Movement Experiences* (Minneapolis, MN: Burgess Publishing Company, 1977).

Herbert M. Greenberg, *Teaching with Feeling* (New York: Macmillan Co., 1969).

G. E. R. Holloway, *The Child's Conception of Space* (London: Routledge & Kegan Paul, published in conjunction with the National Froebel Foundation, 1967).

ERIC HOYLE, *The Role of the Teacher*, Student's Library of Education (London: Routledge & Kegan Paul, 1969).

MARIE HUGHES, *When Teachers Teach* (Washington, D.C.: Association for Childhood Education International, 1966).

J. HUNT, *Intelligence and Experience* (New York: Ronald Press, 1961).

JAMES L. HYMES, JR., "The Importance of Pre-Primary Education." In Rasmussen (Ed.), *Readings from Childhood Education* (Washington, DC: Association for Childhood Education International, 1966).

ELIZABETH JONES, "Teacher Education: Entertainment or Interaction?" (*The Journal of the National Association for the Education of Young Children*, March 1978).

GERALD KENYON, *Value Held for Physical Activity by Selected Urban Secondary School Students in Canada, Australia, England and the United States.* Unpublished, 1968.

HERBERT KOHL, *On Teaching* (New York: Schocken Books, 1976).

MARIA MONTESSORI, *The Montessori Method* (New York: Frederick A. Stokes, 1912).

PHILIP PHENIX, *Perceptions of an Ethicist about the Affective.* (Washington, D.C.: Association for Supervision and Curriculum Development, 1977).

LOUIS RATHS, *Meeting the Needs of Children; Creating Trust and Security* (Columbus, OH: Charles E. Merrill Publishing Co., 1972).

JEAN and SIMONNE SAUVY, *The Child's Discovery of Space* (Baltimore, MD: Penguin Education, 1974).

MYRTLE SCOTT and SADIE GRIMETT (Eds.), *Current Issues in Child Development* (Washington, D.C.: National Association for the Education of Young Children, 1977).

DARYL SIEDENTOP, *Physical Education: Introductory Analysis* (2nd ed.) (Dubuque, IA: William C. Brown Co., 1976).

STEVEN SILVERN and JON WILES, "What Do Early Childhood Principles Imply for the Middle School?" (*Journal of the Association for Supervision and Curriculum Development*, May 1978).

BERNARD SPODEK (Ed.), *Teacher Education of the Teacher, by the Teacher, for the Child* (Washington, D.C.: National Association for the Education of Young Children, 1974).

E. STONES and S. MORRIS, *Teaching Practice, Problems and Perspectives* (London: Methuen and Co., Ltd., 1972).

MARION FENWICK STUART, *Neurophysiological Insights into Teaching* (Palo Alto, CA: Pacific Book Publishers, 1967).

HERBERT A. THELEN, *Education and the Human Quest* (New York: Harper and Brothers, 1960).

Selma Wassermann, "Key Vocabulary: Impact on Beginning Teaching" (*Young Children, Journal of the National Association of Education of Young Children, 33*, no. 3, May 1978).

Chapter 11

Joe L. Frost and Michael L. Henniger, "Making Playgrounds Safe for Children and Children Safe for Playgrounds" (*Young Children, Journal of the National Association for the Education of Young Children, 34*, no. 5, July 1979).

V. Hunt, J. Grenzeback and B. Egle, *Movement Education for Preschool Programs* (Olivette, MO: National Program on Early Childhood Education, 1972).

Chapter 13

Note: These texts were developed to use with older children, but many of the activities are applicable to younger ones if they are presented simply enough. Children, particularly in the gymnasium, are far more capable than we had supposed, so these activities do not become watered-down elementary-school ones but viable body awareness activities that facilitate motor development and challenge the children.

Larry Albertson, "A Motor Development Program for Young Children" (*Physical Educator*, December 1976).

A., Bilbrough and P. Jones, *Physical Education in the Primary School* (London: The University of London Press, 1968).

Don Buckland, *Gymnastics Activity in the Primary School* (London: Heinemann Educational Books, Ltd., 1969).

Department of Education and Science, *Movement Physical Education in the Primary Years* (London: Her Majesty's Stationery Office, 1972).

David Gallahue, *Developmental Play Equipment for Home and School* (New York: John Wiley & Sons, Inc., 1975).

Bonnie Gilliom, *Basic Movement Education for Children* (Reading, MA: Addison-Wesley, 1970).

Jacqueline Herkowitz, "Movement Experiences for Preschool Children" (*Journal of Physical Education and Recreation, 48*, no. 3, November 1978).

———, "Structuring the Movement Environment for Pre-school Children" (*Quest Monograph, XXIV*, 1975).

SANDRA HICKS, "Basic Movement: Building a Foundation for Educational Gymnastics " (Journal of Physical Education and Recreation, June 1979).

VALERIE HUNT, J. GRENZEBACK, and B. EGLE, Movement Education for Preschool Programs (Olivette, MO: National Program on Early Childhood Education, 1972).

DIANA JORDAN, Childhood and Movement (Oxford, England: Basil Blackwell, 1966).

SYBIL KRITCHEVSKY and ELIZABETH PRESCOTT, with LEE WALLING, Planning Environment for Young Children Physical Space (Washington, D.C.: National Association for the Education of Young Children, 1977).

JOHN LEARMOUTH and KEITH WHITAKER, Movement in Practice (Boston, MA: Play, Inc., 1977).

London County Council, Educational Gymnastics (London: The London County Council, 1963).

BETTY LOWNDES, Movement and Creative Drama for Children (Boston: Play Inc., 1971).

BRUCE McCLENAGHAN and DAVID GALLAHUE, Fundamental Movement Observation and Evaluation (Philadelphia: W.B. Saunders, 1978).

MUSKA MOSSTON, Developmental Movement (Columbus, OH: Charles E. Merrill, 1966).

MARCELLA V. RIDENOUR (Ed.), Motor Development; Issues and Applications (Princeton, N.J.: Princeton Book Company, 1978).

MAIDA L. RIGGS, "A Preschool Laboratory Gym" (Journal of Physical Education and Recreation, February 1979).

CAROLINE B. SINCLAIR, Movement of the Young Child: Ages Two to Six (Columbus, OH: Charles E. Merrill, 1973).

JEANNE SNODGRASS, "Self-Concept" (Journal of Physical Education and Recreation, November–December 1977).

MARY HELEN VANIER and DAVID GALLAHUE, Teaching Physical Education in Elementary Schools (Philadelphia: W. B. Saunders Co., 1978).

PETER H. WERNER, A Movement Approach to Games for Children (St. Louis, MO: The C.V. Mosby Company, 1979).

———. "Movement Experience for Preschool Children," (Physical Education, 32, no. 4, 1977).

PETER WERNER and RICHARD SIMMONS, Inexpensive Physical Education Equipment for Children (Minneapolis, MN: Burgess Publishing Company, 1976).

Sources of Indoor and Outdoor
Play Equipment

Children's Education Corporation
20 Kilmer Road
Edison, N.J. 08817

Community Playthings
Rifton, N.Y. 12471

Environmental Structures
Chatsworth, CA 91311

Holbrook Patterson
170 South Monroe Street
Coldwater, MI 49036

North American Recreation
P.O. Box 758
Bridgeport, CT 06601

Playground Corporation of America
29–16 40th Avenue
Long Island City, N.Y. 11101

R. E. Austin and Son
705 Bedford Avenue
Bellmore, N.Y. 11710

Skill Development Equipment
P.O. Box 6300
Anaheim, CA 92807

Index